CRITICAL RESEARCH AND EVALUATION

ROBERT P. NESTOR

University Press of America, Inc.
Lanham • New York • Oxford

Copyright © 2001 by
University Press of America,® Inc.
4720 Boston Way
Lanham, Maryland 20706

12 Hid's Copse Rd.
Cumnor Hill, Oxford OX2 9JJ

Library of Congress Cataloging-in-Publication Data

Nestor, Robert P.
Critical research and evaluation / Robert P. Nestor.
p.   cm
Includes bibliographical references.
1. Research—Methodology—Study and teaching.
2. Research—Evaluation. I. Title.
LB1047.3 .N47 2001   370'.7'2—dc21   2001041487 CIP

ISBN 0-7618-2068-X (pbk. : alk. paper)

Contents

Introduction   1

   Part I   2
   The Parts of a Research Report   3
   Nine Basic Methods of Research   8

Chapter 1
Historical Study—The Mirage of Immortality
by *Arnold J. Toynbee*   11

   Useful List of Criteria for Conducting a Critical
   Analysis of Research Studies   17

Chapter 2
Descriptive Study—Do Grades Stimulate Students to Failure?
by *Charles H. Josephson*   19

   Do "Good" Students Want to Fail?   20
   Compliance with Group Demands Not Conscious for Majority   20
   Students Divided by School into Three Groups   21
   Questions Designed to Insure Honesty   22
   Combining Higher Groups Produces Disturbing Picture   22
   Grade Aspirations Reflect Motivation   23
   Results Raise Doubts About Grading System   24
   No Good Subject For Grades Available   24
   Ability Grouping May Encourage Failure   25
   Average Students Have Lowest Aspiration Level   25
   Useful List of Criteria for Conducting a Critical Analysis
      of Research Studies   26

Chapter 3
Quasi-Experimental Study—"Head Start" Experience and the
Development of Skills and Abilities in Kindergarten Children
by *Eleanor S. Kaplan*   29

    Introduction   30
    Procedure   37
    Results   41
    Discussion   49
    Summary   51
    Useful List of Criteria for Conducting a Critical
        Analysis of Research Studies 52

Chapter 4
An Introduction to Qualitative/Ethnographic Research   55

    Self Training Exercise   57
    Analysis of Data   59
    General Interview Techniques   60
    Characteristics of Qualitative and Quantitative Research 62

Chapter 5
Qualitative Study—The West End: An Urban Village
by *Herbert Gans*   71

    Overview   71
    Life in the West End   72
    The Italians of the West End   73
    The Structure of West End Society: An Introduction
        to the Peer Group Society 73
    The Individual and the Group   76
    Suggested Questions for Evaluating a Qualitative Study—
        in this case—Participant Observation 82

Chapter 6
Evaluation Research   85

    Types of Evaluation   85
    Stages in Conducting Evaluation Research   86
    How You Go About Conducting Evaluation Research   87

Chapter 7
Evaluation Studies—Dropout Factors in the Process of
Influencing Classroom Change Through Teacher Education
by *Ladd Holt and Don Uhlenberg*   91

    Evaluation Study   91
    Background and Purpose   92
    Dropout Factors   94
    Procedures and Results   95
    Conclusions and Implications   101

Chapter 8
The Relationship Between Type of Teacher Reinforcement
and Student Inquiry Behavior in Science
by *Clifford H. Edwards and Michael Burma*   103

    Introduction   103
    Method   105
    Procedure   106
    Results   108
    Discussion   109

Chapter 9
The Research Problem—Conditions to Help in Selecting a Problem   111

    Null Hypothesis   114
    Structuring Your Research Activities   114
    Problem Presentation   115
    Sources of Problems   116
    Building Researchable Problems   117
    Elements of a Research Proposal   119
    A Survey Technique   120
    The Letter of Transmittal   122

Appendix A
An Author's Critique: "Head Start"—The Development of
Skills, Experience, and Abilities in Kindergarten Children   125

Appendix B
An Author's Critique: "The West End"—An Urban Village   133

References   147

Introduction

I n the educational setting which many a student encounters, there are disciplines that are often mastered by collecting and memorizing a series of facts. In research, one applies a methodology to a wide variety of situations in order to arrive at a meaningful interpretation of some phenonenon or setting under study. Research is, in effect, an art of applying a set of skills in solving a researchable problem. Such a stated goal often gives both student and teacher a great deal of difficulty when the development of research skills must conform to the time limitation of one semester or one or two courses in research.

Most texts in research aim at the production of research. To produce a research study in one semester often causes a finished product with a great deal of limitations or a "need for further study" emphasized in the conclusion section of the paper. The present text aims at introducing the research process, as well as attempting to help the student understand enough of its skills (in conjunction with other texts) so that he or she may "read" a research report intelligently. This book aims at providing opportunities for active engagement in the critical description of completed research and the design of student initiated studies by looking at what others have done. The research process should become much more meaningful to those who have same direct, personal use for its skills than when it is studied in isolation.

Part I of the text appeals to the student as a lifetime "consumer" of research results. Consuming research provides a strong foundation for the decision-making that every professional must do in his or her professional role. For example, recently a department of education in a southwestern state published an attractive report about a large-scale pilot study concerning the effectiveness of a special instructional technique. The report included glowing testimonials from many teachers who had

1

field-tested the new method. Several persons who saw the positive statements failed to notice that the results showed almost no difference between subjects in the treatment and control groups. Some of the readers
even decided to use the new method. As this example illustrates, it is
particularly important as a consumer of research to be thorough in your
analysis of research if you plan to apply the results to your own setting.

In Part I, you will become acquainted with a brief summary of commonly used research methods. This will be followed by a series of articles illustrating the various research methods in a real setting. You will
be asked to critique those articles using a list of relevant criteria. It is
hoped that the exercise involved in dissecting those research articles will
pay the relevant benefit of some research experience when you under-
take your own research efforts.

Part II of the book deals with Evaluation Research with the assumption that today's educator or social science worker will, at some point in
his or her career, be the subject of or be actively involved in evaluation
research. The theory, as well as practical strategies involving evaluation
research, will be discussed.

Part III of Critical Research and Evaluation will delve into the elements of a research proposal with an outline of questions that should be
answered when writing a research proposal whether for a course or dis-
sertation or for the funding of a particular project with grant money.

Part I

Research is the application of the scientific method to the investigation
of some problem of interest to the researcher. To carry out this approach, a careful sequence of actions called the stages of research is
commonly employed. One becomes aware of the problem (or felt difficulty), defines the problem (keeping in mind that any definition must be
operationalized or made measurable), develops hypotheses (educated guess
as to its solution), tests the hypotheses (gathers relevant data) and
draws.conclusions about the test results (analyzes the data and interprets
meaning in relation to the problem and hypothesis one started out with).
'Research is useful both as a process and as a product. As a process,
research tests theories or parts of theories to create knowledge. As a
product, reported research can provide insight and help in understanding
life. Reports of such research efforts are commonly available from many

sources. The format of such reports contain the following main parts: an abstract (usually an abbreviated version of a research report), an introduction, the method used in the study, the results, and discussion. In the articles contained in this section, you will learn how to analyze and evaluate the information contained in the research reports. The ideal way of doing that would be in a group setting where an interchange of interpretations would lead to a consensus on what actually was reported in the article and whether or not the article met the expectations of criteria that have been established to evaluate a given article in a critical fashion.

The purpose of this section will be to give you some guidelines against which to judge the quality of the product that is often offered to the public for consumption. It should help you to ask intelligent questions about the production of a given research effort, to inspect its design and procedures, to examine the validity of its conclusions so that you may be better able to judge the value of the research, appraise its worth intelligently and avoid the pitfalls when you conduct your own research study.

The Parts of a Research Report

1. The title and other heading material. The report usually begins with a title, stating the subject with which the report will deal. The name of the researcher and professional affiliation is also a part of the title material.
2. An abstract of the reported research. Many research reports begin with an abstract, some do not. The abstract gives a summary or overview of the entire research endeavor. This part of the report assists the reader to get a miniature reporting of the entire project, thus helping the reader to decide whether he wishes to read further.
3. The introduction. The introduction to the report proper usually consists of a paragraph, or several paragraphs, which aim to give some justification for the research being reported. It may include a review of antecedent research by others, the significance of the research which is being reported, an indication of its importance or relevance to existing practical problems, and its relation to other existing research.
4. The statement of the research goal. Every report should set forth clearly, either by obvious implication or by direct statement, the problem which forms the heart of the research effort. What was the

researcher attempting to do? What is the problem for which he was seeking a solution? What undiscovered knowledge was he trying to find? What was the purpose of the research project? The report should set forth the problem clearly so that we have no doubt as to what the researcher was attempting to do.

Carefully written research reports always inform the reader precisely what the problem was that has been researched. This is one of the first items to look for when reading any reporting of research. Failure to delineate the problem clearly for the reader reflects upon the quality of the report, but more seriously it hints at the ability of the researcher writing the report to think without confusion clearly—to put first things first. Language is the mirror of the mind. Reports that ramble, that fail to zoom in, isolating the central research objective, setting it forth appropriately and adequately in unmistakable terms, unfortunately raise a presumption that the quality of the research itself may have a possible kinship with the verbal fog found in the report. Reportorial haze should alert you to read the rest of the report with circumspection and with more than usual care.

5. Related research. Throughout the report, and especially in the introductory section, the efforts of others are acknowledged and their relevancy to the research being reported is indicated. Those who engage in research are quite cognizant that the work of others assists them in resolving their own problem. No research effort is ever an isolated quest.

The manner in which reference to related research is indicated varies, but, in general, there are two major types of reference. Sometimes reference to the work of others is noted by employing a number—usually in parentheses—following the citation. This number refers to the comparably numbered item in the list of references at the end of the report.

Related research literature references may also use a different style: the name or names of the researchers, followed by the year of publication of their research report.

6. The method and design of the research. The research method is the way in which the researcher gathers the data and analyzes them so that they will reveal their meaning. We shall list briefly the various methods of research with a brief explanation of each. While research methodology goes under a variety of names, basic processes by which data are processed may be described under four general headings.

(a) The descriptive, or normative, survey method. Employing this method, the researcher gathers data by observation or by surveying the research universe and/or population, and then, usually by means of simple statistics, seeks to discover what the data seem to indicate.

(b) The statistical-analysis method. This method of gathering and processing the data employs statistics—usually inferential statistics—to force the data to reveal their meaning.

(c) The experimental method. In the experimental method, one group of subjects is controlled by the researcher, while another and similar group is submitted to some influence, called a variable. The data of the two groups are then compared to determine whether the addition of the variable has had any effect on the outcome. If the experimental group—the group subjected to the variable—differs from the control group—the group that had nothing done to them—then it can be presumed that the variable is responsible for the difference between the two groups.

(d) The historical method. In this method, the data are usually in the form of historical records or documents: Letters, records of events, diaries, written memoranda, artifacts, or other documentary remains. Given these documents, the historical method seems to inspect them critically so that from these documentary data, unsolved historical or philosophical problems may be resolved or new facts of historical importance discovered.

In the research report, under the heading of method, many researchers also report other items, two of the most common of which are a description of the subjects used in the research project and the method employed in their selection. A discussion of the procedure used to collect, process, and interpret the data as well as other matters may also be introduced under the heading of "method." These may include the criteria which have been used for the admissibility of data into the study, the precautions which have been taken to safeguard against contamination of the data by the influence of bias, or other precautions which have been taken to insure objectivity and impartiality in the study. These are all appropriate considerations under the heading of method or under any of its subheadings. And the careful researcher will usually delineate somewhere in his report his safeguarding of the integrity of the study by noting these matters.

Sometimes, under the general heading of method, researchers discuss the way in which they have gathered the data, the instruments employed, the materials used, or corollary studies which have provided standards or evaluate scales for the processing of the data. Under method, in fact, any facts pertinent to the initiation or the execution of the study may be appropriately discussed.

7. The results. In this section, the researcher sets forth the interpretations which the data seem to warrant. If the research was guided by hypotheses, here is where a statement is made as to whether the data supported or rejected those hypotheses. In statistical studies where the the null hypothesis is tested, the statistical value established for either accepting or rejecting the hypothesis is given and the reader is advised whether the hypothesis was confirmed or rejected.

8. The discussion. The discussion section of a research report frequently contains a brief recapitulation of the entire research process. Here also the problem which formed the basis for the research endeavor is resolved. The conclusions—warranted by the data—are stated. The researcher may suggest the applicability of the research findings to specific life situations, or note other conclusions which are ancillary to the main problem but which the data way have revealed and are significant enough to merit comment.

Concluding the discussion section, suggestions for additional projects which may supplement the research being reported may also be offered.

9. Notes and references. The final section of any research report is a listing of the documentary sources indicated within the body of the report. Within this listing may be items that are either comments of the author or informational footnotes. They are there to amplify the discussion but have no documentary reference quality.

The following considerations regarding the way research is communicated should enter into your analysis when you critique the research reports contained in this section of our text.

1. There are three types of arguments advanced for the internal and external validity of the findings of a research project. In

order of their conconsidered strength, they are: reasoning, methods, and replications.

2. Because of space constraints, researchers rarely include everything that was done in the conduct of the research in the written report. Omissions can affect the accurary of the material's interpretation.

3. Educators need to possess the skills necessary for reading and interpreting research reports.

4. Research reports should be written as an objective description or opinion, without elaborate and complicated sentence structure. Clear writing in research would aim at producing the precise word, avoid ambiguity, present ideas in an orderly fashion and avoid grammar or words that distract from major points.

5. Results should be presented objectively, without interpretation, and should provide an overview of general patterns in the results.

6. Inferential type results must be accompanied by descriptive statistics, be presented without interpretation or elaboration, give information about the test employed, and state the level of significance of the results.

7. Qualitative type research results are presented as verbal analysis and are written at different levels of generalization or abstraction based upon the object of the study and the methods employed.

8. Interpreting the results of the study involves a subjective analysis of the results based on the type of research design used and the findings of the previous research.

9. Interpretations based on previous research usually confirm or contradict previous studies. If results prove contradictory, explanation should be provided in the discussion section of the report.

10. Conclusions about the study are expected to be summary statements based on the results and on the initial research problem. The conclusion section should state the limitations and the generalizability of the research as well as any need for further research.

Nine Basic Methods of Research

Method 1	Purpose
Historical	To reconstruct the past objectively and accurately, often in relation to the tenability of an hypothesis.

Example

A study reconstructing practices in the teaching of spelling in the United States during the past fifty years; tracing the history of civil rights in the United States system of education since the civil war; testing the hypothesis that Francis Bacon is the real author of the "works of William Shakespeare."

Method 2	Purpose
Descriptive	To describe systematically a situation or area of interest factually and accurately.

Example

Population census studies, public opinion surveys, fact-finding surveys, status studies, task analysis studies, questionnaire and interview studies, observation studies, job descriptions, surveys of the literature, documentary analyses, anecdotal records, critical incident reports, test score analyses, and normative data.

Method 3	Purpose
Developmental	To investigate patterns and sequences of growth and/or changes as a function of time.

Example

A longitudinal growth study following an initial sample of 200 children from six months of age to adulthood; a cross-sectional growth study investigating changing patterns of intelligence by sampling groups of children at different age levels; a trend study projecting the future growth and educational needs of a community from past trends and recent building estimates.

Method 4	Purpose
Case and Field	To study intensively the background, current status and environmental interactions of a given social unit; an individual, group, institution, or community.

Example

The case history of a child with an above average IQ but with learning disabilities; an intensive study of a group of teenage youngsters on probation for drug abuse; an intensive study of a typical suburban community in the Midwest in terms of its socio-economic characteristics.

Method 5	**Purpose**
Correlational	To investigate the extent to which variations in one factor correspond with variations in one or more other factors based on correlation coefficients.

Example

To investigate relationships between reading achievement scores and one or more other variables of interest; a factor-analytic study of several intelligence tests; a study to predict success in college based on intercorrelation patterns between college grades and selected high school variables.

Method 6	**Purpose**
Casual-Comparative or "Ex Post Facto"	To investigate possible cause-and-effect relationships by observing some existing consequence and searching back through the data for plausible causal factors.

Example

To identify factors related to the "drop-out" problem in a particular high school using data from records over the past ten years; to investigate similarities and differences between such groups as smokers and nonsmokers, readers and nonreaders, or delinquents and nondelinquents, using data on file.

Method 7	**Purpose**
True Experimental	To investigate possible cause-and-effect relationships by exposing one or more experimental groups to one or more treatment conditions and comparing the results to one or more control groups not receiving the treatment (random assignment being essential).

Example

To investigate.the effectiveness of three methods of teaching reading to first grade children using random assignments of children and teachers to groups and methods; to investigate the effects of a specific tranquilizing drug on the learning behavior of boys identified as "hyperactive" using random assignment to groups receiving three different levels of the drug and two control groups with and without a placebo, respectively.

Method 8	**Purpose**
Quasi-Experimental	To approximate the conditions of the true experiment in a setting which does not allow the control and/or manipulation of all relevant variables. The researcher must clearly understand what compromises exist in the internal and external validity of his design and proceed within these limitations.

Example

Most so-called field experiments, operational research, and even the more sophisticated forms of action research which attempt to get at causal factors in real life settings where only partial control is possible; e.g., an investigation of the effectiveness of any method or treatment condition where random assignment of subjects to methods or conditions is not possible.

Method 9	**Purpose**
Action	To develop new skills or new approaches and to solve problems with direct application to the classroom or other applied setting.

Example

An inservice training program to help teachers develop new skills in facilitating class discussions; to experiment with new approaches to teaching reading to bilingual children; to develop more effective counseling techniques for underchievers.

Chapter 1

Historical Study—
The Mirage of Immortality

ARNOLD J. TOYNBEE*

If we look at these universal states, not as alien observers but through the eyes of their own citizens, we shall find that these not only desire that these earthly commonwealths of theirs should live forever but actually believe that the immortality of these human institutions is assured, and this sometimes in the teeth of contemporary events which, to an observer posted at a different standpoint in time or space, declare beyond question that this particular universal state is at that very moment in its last agonies. Why is it, such an observer might well ask, that, in defiance of apparently plain facts, the citizens of a universal state are prone to regard it, not as a night's shelter in the wilderness, but as the Promised Land, the goal of human endeavors? It should be said, however, that this sentiment is confined to the citizens of universal states established by indigenous empire-builders. No Indian, for example, either desired or foretold the immortality of the British Raj.

In the history of the Roman Empire, which was the universal state of the Hellenic civilization, we find the generation that had witnessed the establishment of the Pax Augusta asserting, in evidently sincere good

* Arnold J. Toynbee, A Study of History, abridged ed., Oxford University Press, New York, 1957, vol.11, pp.4-6, 8-10. Reprinted by permission.

faith, that the Empire and the City that had built it have been endowed with a common immortality. Tibullus (circa 54-18 B.C.) sings of "the walls of the eternal city" while Virgil (70-19 B.C.) makes his Iuppiter, speaking of the future Roman scions of Aeneas' race, say: "I give them empire without end." Livy writes with the same assurance of "the city founded for eternity." Horace, sceptic though he was, in claiming immortality for his Odes, takes as his concrete measure of eternity the repetition of the annual round of the religious ritual of the Roman city state, The Odes are still alive on the lips of men. How much longer their "immortality" will continue is uncertain, for the number of those who can quote them has been sadly diminished in recent times by changes in educational fashions; but at least they have lived four or five times as long as the Roman pagan ritual. More than four hundred years after the age of Horace and Virgil, after the sack of Rome by Alaric has already announced the end, we find the Gallic poet Rutilus Namatianus still defiantly asserting Rome's immortality and Saint Jerome, in scholarly retreat at Jerusalem, interrupting his theological labours to express his grief and stupefaction in language almost identical with that of Ruitilus. The pagan official and the Christian Father are united in their emotional reactions to an event which, as we now see it, had been inevitable for generations.

The shock administered by the fall of Rome in A.D.410 to the citizens of a transient universal state which they had mistaken for an everlasting habitation has its counterpart in the shock suffered by the subjects of the Arab Caliphate when Baghdad fell to the Mongols in A.D.1258. In the Roman world the shock was felt from Palestine to Gaul; in the Arab world from Farghanah to Andalsia.

The intensity of the psychological effect is even more remarkable in this than in the Roman case; for, by the time when Hulagu gave the "Abbasid Caliphate its coup de grace, its sovereign had been ineffective for three or four centuries over the greater part of the vast domain nominally subject to it. This halo of the illusory immortality, worn by moribund universal states, often persuades the more prudent barbarian leaders, in the very act of parcelling out their dominions among themselves, to acknowledge an equally illusory subjection. The Amulung leaders of the Arian Ostrogoths and the Buwayhid leaders of the Shii Daylamis sought title for their conquests by ruling them, in official theory, as viceregents of the Emperor at Constantinople and the Caliph at Baghdad respectively; and, though this tactful handling of a senile universal state did not avail, in their case, to avert the doom to which both these warbands condemned themselves by clinging to their distinctive religious heresies, the same political manoeuvre was brilliantly successful when executed by fellow barbarians who had the sagacity or good fortune to be at the same time impeccable in their professions of religious faith. Clovis the Frank, for example, the most successful of all the founders of barbarian successor-states of the Roman Empire, followed-up his conversion to Catholicism by obtaining from the Emperor Anastasius in distant Constantinople the title of proconsul with consular insignia. His success is attested by the fact that in later ages not less than eighteen royal Louis, reigning in the land that he conquered, bore a modified variant of his name.

The Ottoman Empire, which became the universal state of a Byzantine civilization, exhibited the same characteristics of illusory immortality at a time when it had already become "the Sick Man of Europe." The ambitious warlords who were carving out for themselves successor-states—a Mehmed 'Ali in Egypt and Syria, an "Ali of Yannina in Albania and Greece, and a Pasvanoghlu of Viddin in the northwestern corner of Rumelia—were sedulous in doing in the Padishah's name all that they were doing to his detriment in their own private interests. When the Western Powers followed in their footsteps, they adopted the same fictions. Great Britain, for example, administered Cyprus from 1878 and Egypt from 1882 in the name of the Sultan at Constantinople until she found herself at war with Turkey in 1914.

The Mughal universal state of the Hindu civilization displays the same features. Within half a century of the Emperor Awrangzib's death in A.D. 1707, an empire which had once exercised effective sovereignty over the greater part of the Indian subcontinent had been whittled down to a torso some 250 miles long and 100 miles broad. After another half-century it had been reduced to the circuit of the walls of the Red Fort at Delhi. Yet, 150 years after A.D. 1707, a descendant of Akbar and Awrangzib was still squatting on their throne, and might have been left there much longer if the mutineers of 1857 had not forced this poor puppet, against his wishes, to give his blessing to their revolt against a raj from overseas which had, after a period of anarchy, replaced the long-extinct Mughal Raj which he still symbolized.

A still more remarkable testimoney to the tenacity of the belief in the immortality of universal states is the practice of evoking their ghosts after they have proved themselves mortal by expiring. The 'Abbasid

Caliphate of Baghdad was thus resuscitated in the shape of the Holy Roman Empire of the West and the East Roman Empire of Orthodox Christendom; and the empire of the Ts'in and Han dynasties in the shape of the Sui and T'ang Empire of the Far Eastern civilization. The surname of the founder of the Roman Empire was revived in the titles Kaiser and Czar, and the title of Caliph, which originally meant successor of Muhammad, after haunting Cairo, passed on to Istanbul, where it survived until its abolition at the hands of Westernizing revolutionists in the twentieth century.

These are only a selection from the wealth of historical examples illustrating the fact that the belief in the immortality of universal states survives for centuries after it has been confuted by plain hard facts. What are the causes of this strange phenomenon?

One manifest cause is the potency of the impression made by the founders and the great rulers of universal states, an impression handed on to a receptive posterity with an emphasis which exaggerates an imposing truth into an overwhelming legend. Another cause is the impressiveness of the institution itself, apart from the genius displayed by its greatest rulers.

And yet the reality of these universal states was something very different from the brilliant surface that they presented to Aelius Aristeides and their other panegyrists in various ages and various climes.

An obscure divinity of the Nubian marches of the Egyptiac universal state was transfigured by the genius of Hellenic mythology into a mortal king of the Ethiopians who had the misfortune to be loved by Eos, the immortal Goddess of the Dawn. The goddess besought her fellow Olympians to confer on her human lover the immortality which she and her peers enjoyed; and, jealous though they were of their divine privileges, she teased them into yielding at last to her feminine importunity. Yet even this grudging gift was marred by a fatal flaw; for the eager goddess had forgotten that the Olympians' immortality was mated with an everlasting youth, and the other immortals had spitefully taken care to grant her no more than her bare request. The consequence was both ironic and tragic. After a honeymoon that flashed past in the twinkling of an Olympian eye, Eos and her now immortal but still inexorably ageing mate found themselves condemned for eternity to grieve together over Tithonus's hapless plight. A senility to which the merciful hand of death could never set a term was an affliction that no mortal man could ever be made to suffer, and an eternal grief was an obsession that left no room for any other thought or feeling.

For any human soul or human institution an immortality in This World would prove a martyrdom, even if it were unaccompanied by either physical decrepitude or mental senility. "In this sense," wrote the philosophic Emperor Marcus Aurelius (A.D.161-180), "it would be true to say that any man of forty who is endowed with moderate intelligence has seen—in the light of the uniformity of Nature—the entire Past and Future"; and, if this estimate of the capacity of human souls for experience strikes the reader as an inordinately low one, he may find the reason in the age in which Marcus lived; for an "Indian Summer" is an age of boredom. The price of the Roman Peace was the forfeiture of Hellenic liberty; and, though that liberty might always have turned irresponsible and oppressive, it was manifest in retrospect that the turbulent wickedness of the Ciceronian climax of an Hellenic "Time of Troubles" had provided a wealth of exciting and inspiring themes for Roman public speakers which their epigoni in a smugly ordered Trajanic epoch might conventionally condemn as horrors, not nostri sacculi, but must secretely envy as they found themselves perpetually failing in their laborious efforts to substitute far-fetched artifice for the stimulus of importunate life.

On the morrow of the breakdown of the Hellenic society Plato, anxiously seeking to safeguard it against a further fall by pegging it in a securely rigid posture, had idealized the comparative stability of the Egyptiac culture; and a thousand years later, when this Egyptiac culture was still in being while the Hellenic civilization had arrived at its last agonies, the last of the Neoplatonists pushed their reputed master's sentiment to an almost frenzied pitch of uncritical admiration.

Thanks to the obstanacy of the Egyptiac universal state in again and again insisting on returning to life after its body had been duly laid on the salutary funeral pyre, the Egyptiac civilization lived to see its contemporaries—the Minoan, the Sumeric, and the Indus culture—all pass away and give place to successors of a younger generation, some of which had passed away in their turn while the Egyptiac society still kept alive. Egyptiac students of history could have observed the birth and death of the First Syriac, Hittite, and Babylonig offspring of the Sumeric civilization and the rise and decline of the Syriac and Hellenic offspring of the Minoan. Yet the fabulously long-drawn-out epilogue to the broken-down Egyptiac society's natural term of life was but an alternation of long stretches of boredom with hectic bouts of demonic energy, into which this somnolent society was galvanized by the impact of alien bodies social.

The same rhythm of trance-like somnolence alternating with outbursts of fanatical xenophobia can be discerned in the epilogue to the history of the Far Eastern civilization in China. The tincture of Far Eastern Christian culture in the Mongols who had forced upon China an alien universal state evoked a reaction in which the Mongols were evicted and their dominion replaced by the indigenous universal state of the Ming. Even the Manchu barbarians, who stepped into the political vacuum created by the Ming's collapse, and whose taint of Far Eastern Christian culture was less noticeable than their receptivity in adopting the Chinese way of life, aroused a popular opposition which, in Southern China at any rate, never ceased to maintain itself underground and broke out into the open again in the Taiping insurrection of A.D. 1852-64. The infiltration of the Early Modern Western civilization, in its Catholic Christian form in the sixteenth and seventeenth centuries provoked the proscription of Catholicism in the first quarter of the eighteenth century. The blasting open of the seagates of China for Western trade between A.D. 1839 and A.D. 1861 provoked the retort of the anti-Western "Boxer" rising of A.D. 1900; and the Manchu Dynasty was overthrown in A.D. 1911 in retribution for the double crime of being ineradicably alien itself and at the same time showing itself imcompetent to keep the now far more formidable alien force of Western penetration at bay.

Happily, life is kinder than legend, and the sentence of immortality which mythology passed on Tithonus is commuted, for the benefit of the universal states of history, to a not interminable longevity. Marcus's disillusioned man of forty must die at last though he may outlive his zest for life by fifty or sixty years, and a universal state that kicks again and again against the pricks of death will weather away in the course of ages, like the pillar of salt that was fabled to be the petrified substance of a once living woman.

Useful List of Criteria for Conducting a Critical Analysis of Research Studies

I. The People Involved

- Were the subjects described adequately?
- Who were the subjects in the sample?
- How many?
- How was the sample chosen?
- What population does the sample represent?
- To what group could conclusions be generalized?
- Were the rights of the subjects violated? (Invasion of privacy/coercion etc.)
- Would the subjects benefit from the research?

II. Purpose of the Research

- What is the purpose of the research?
- Where did the purpose of the research originate?
- What is the specific problem statement?
- Was the purpose or problem clearly stated?
- Who sponsored the research?
- How and by whom were the questions generated?
- What is the relationship of the problem to previous research knowledge?
- Was the argument logical?

II. Methodology

- What research methodology was employed?
- Was the methodology appropriate to the purpose of the problem?
- Were the variables measured? How were the variables measured?
- Was the measurement of the variables adequate?
- Issue of objectivity vs. subjectivity?
- Under what conditions was the research conducted?
- Was the analysis of the data adequate?

IV. Results

- What were the results?
- What can and cannot be concluded from the results?
- How accessible are results? To whom?
- Do the results follow from the methodology?
- Is data, upon which results are based, accessible?
- How will research results be used?
- Were the limitations of the research clearly stated?
- Are conclusions clearly stated?
- Is the need for further research stated or evident?

V. Underlying Assumptions

- Definitions (stated or implied)?
- (learning, education, motivation, development, growth are examples of terms that might be defined in light of a particular study).
- Did you detect any *bias* of the researcher?
- Could researcher bias contaminate the study?
- What assumptions are implicit in the research methodology used?
- What other underlying assumptions are implied in this research study?

Chapter 2

Descriptive Study—Do Grades Stimulate Students to Failure?*

Charles H. Josephson

Nearly fifteen years ago Allison Davis took the position that students in slum schools may well find it more rewarding to be considered academic failures than to be successes in school.[1]

If false, this observation should not go unchallenged; if true it should not be unheeded. The reason is simple: this observation washes away the underpinnings of one of the primary official sanctions traditionally used by the teacher and the school to direct pupil behavior.

All teachers offer promise of high grades as a reward for learning and promise of low grades as a punishment for failure. What irony there would be if we found a situation in which the teacher's reward has become the student's punishment—a situation in which the student is actually motivated to "achieve" in the direction the teacher regards as "failure."

Do "Good" Students Want to Fail?

To test the validity of Davis' observation, a study was conducted in a high school that serves one of Chicago's lower class neighborhoods.

* Originally appeared in the Chicago Schools Journal, December 1961, pp. 122-127. Reprinted with permission. Published by Chicago State University.

19

Although the group studied was small—only 106 students—and the classification as to level of ability of the students was relatively rough, the results of the study was surprising enough to merit serious consideration. The study began with the hypothesis that, if Davis' observation was true, the students most likely to succeed would feel the strongest pressure to fail. Thus, students of high ability would desire lower grades than students of low ability.

This inversion of values is not intuitively reasonable; we expect high-ability students to desire high grades and low-ability students to be quite happy with low grades. But, for the following reasons, accepting Davis' observation leads logically to an inverse relationship of ability to grade aspirations.

To a large extent, adolescent behavior is peer-oriented; that is, among many forces that determine what the adolescent is likely to do must be included the desire to be accepted by his immediate circle of acquaintances. This involves accepting and following the common values of the group. For example, adolescent groups might include among these values such obvious peculiarities as a fondness for rock-and-roll music, a distinctive hair style, the ability or at least willingness to fight, and so forth.

Compliance with Group Demands
Not Conscious for Majority

However, one is likely to notice that a majority of the group do not consciously comply with group demands. In fact, the existence of such demands may be something of which most group members are not even aware; only those who are violating group values are likely to be conscious of the estrangement the violation brings. For example, if duck-tailed haircuts are highly regarded, only the group members who do not have duck-tails will feel a pressure to develop them. Those group members who have duck-tailed haircuts do not consciously recognize the existence of a pressure for them.

Now, Davis' observation suggests a peculiar value for adolescent groups from the lower classes, namely, low grades in school. The reasons for this—including among others a "natural" rebellion against authority—are far too complex to be included here. Yet if we accept this value as accurately depicting the state of affairs, it would follow that the student who has at one time received high grades will, on entering adolescence, discover that his high grades are inhibiting peer acceptance. Thus, for the gifted student, high grades will come to be negatively perceived, while low grades develop a positive value. But the below-average student, whose low grades represent the summit of his achievement, will not even be aware of this value; in fact, he will wish that his intellectual efforts could be met with a higher reward. Thus he can accept the institutional value which favors high grades, perhaps reflecting his dreams of one day "getting smart" as one put it.

Students Divided by School into Three Groups

It is on this basis that we may hypothesize that in lower-class schools students of low ability will desire high grades, and students of high ability will desire low grades. The laborious task of defining what was included in the word "ability" was eliminated in this instance by assuming that the hierarchy of ability placement that was followed in the subject school was accurate. The school has three main ability groups: roughly 10 per cent of all students are placed in an "accelerated" program; about 50 per cent are in a "regular" plan; about 40 per cent are in a "remedial" program. Although teachers cite individual injustices, most agree that the general rankings are valid. That is, accelerated pupils have "more" ability than regular pupils, who in turn exceed the remedials.

One class was selected from each ability grouping. After a short introduction, primarily assuring that responses would be kept anonymous, four questions were asked:

(1) If you had your choice of any grade for this class, what grade would you select for yourself?
(2) If you could give an imaginary best friend the grade you think he would most like to receive, what grade would you give?
(3) What grade do you feel you deserve in this course?
(4) What grade do you expect to receive in this course?

Table 2.1

Grade Desired	Remedial Class		Regular Class		Accelerated Class	
	Number of Students	Percent of Total	Number of Students	Percent of Total	Number of Students	Percent of Total
1	11	33	8	23	12	31
2	12	37	6	18	13	33
3	9	27	14	41	12	31
4	1	3	6	18	2	5
Totals	33		34		39	

Questions Designed to Insure Honesty

The second question serves as an honesty check on the answer to the first question. One would assume an unwillingness to cooperate on the part of the student whose answer to these two questions differed appreciably. In only one case, in fact, did the response differ by more than one level. The last two questions were to assure that the assumption that achievement does not exceed aspirations would be reasonable for this group. This assumption was needef for certain implications.

The crucial question, of course, is the first. Answers to this question may be tabulated for the three groups as follows (Percents are in rounded figures, and grades are identified as "1" through "5," "1" being high and "5" indicating failure.) See Table 2.1.

Even a cursory examination of the data presented for the three groups makes the conclusion inescapable that in the slightly more than one hundred pupils studied the direct inverse relationship between ability and grades desired does not obtain. However, additional study of the data reveals the possibility that ability groupings may have been made too fine. If regular and accelerated students are classified in a single category (average and above average), and if remedial students are treated as "below average," a significantly different picture emerges.

Combining Higher Groups
Produces Disturbing Picture

Thirty-three per cent of the below average students select as most desirable the grade of "1" (the highest grade); only 27 per cent of the average and above average students select the highest grade. Thirty-seven per cent of the below average select grade "2"; only 26 per cent of the average and above average. Twenty-seven per cent of the below average select grade "3," 36 per cent of the average and above average select "3." Three per cent of the below average group choose grade "4," eleven per cent of the average and above average select the lowest grade offered. None of either group selects grade "5."

Even though such a liberal treatment of the data as this is required for the direct inverse relationship between grade aspirations and ability to become visible, there is cause for concern. Surprisingly, students in the sample obviously do not universally place a high value upon good grades. Moreover, students at and above the average in ability tend to prefer lower grades, as a group, than do students who are below average ability. In fact, note that slightly more than half of the higher ability students would prefer to receive above average grades—assuming "3" to be average. It is not surprising that no students select "5," the failing grade, as a desirable grade; this was expected. What is surprising is that, of the accelerated group of "gifted" students, only a third prefer superior grades; nearly the same number prefer average or below average grades.

Grade Aspirations Reflect Motivation

It is virtually axiomatic in psychological studies of learning that a student will learn primarily what he wants to learn. Hence we place great stress upon motivation, a term that suggests both the "amount of desire" a student possesses for learning a particular knowledge, and the process by which this "desire" may be brought into being or increased. Motivation is not well understood, but its importance under this definition is not disputed.

So far we have been talking about grade aspirations, not motivation. But it seems reasonable to suggest that aspirations, to a degree, reflect motivation; a student who desires a high grade will correspondingly adjust his efforts so that he will receive a grade as high as possible. And a student who envisions low grades as desirable will probably work to receive low grades. Thus, although aspirations do not determine achievement, we may be drawn to the conclusion that they nevertheless limit achievement.

What we are saying is that a student quite possibly will not achieve the grade he most desires, but he certainly will not achieve a grade higher than his aspirations. And the study bears this out. In only one case did a student feel he deserved or would receive a grade higher than the grade to which he aspired—a genuine over-achiever! In more than 75 per cent of the cases, the grade the student felt he deserved was the same or one point below his aspirations. And in more than 65 per cent of the cases the grade the student actually expected to receive was identical with or one point below the grade aspiration.

Results Raise Doubts About Grading System

These interpretations tend to dispute the value of a grading system such as the one followed by the school that was surveyed. This is not the first formal or informal dispute with grading as a means of pupil evaluation. Generally, the concern has been that grading is an inadequate and often an arbitrary means of measuring learning. (In fact, one study has shown that a similar value orientation on the part of the teacher and student will tend to produce good grades more readily than will a student's acquisition of the body of knowledge the teacher presents.) Here, in addition, we seem able to conclude that grading as an evaluating process may actually serve as a deterrent to learning.

Currently, it appears that grading serves basically two functions: to evaluate learning, and to promote learning. As an evaluative tool, the letter grade says to the pupil, "You and your friends have been separated into five categories; you are most like category such-and-so." We need not be surprised or offended if the pupil selects friends of lesser ability and then seeks to join their grading category. As a means of promoting learning, the grade says to the pupil. "Here I am, now chase me!" It has been a dream of educators that all students, particularly the brightest ones, will "chase" the top grades. At least for the subject group, this is false. A specific grade indeed serves as a magnet, but it is not a magnet that draws the best out of the pupil. In fact, it may serve as a stimulus to failure for many students whose ability gives them no right to fail.

No Good Subject For Grades Available

Whether or not the two functions of evaluating and promoting learning make grades an appropriate tool for the teacher may, in the light of this, be open to question. In the years that have passed since Davis observed that we do not know how to properly reward students from lower classes, no widely accepted substitute for a system of grades has been developed. Grades as an administrative tool seem to be here to stay, and the day when a school's legal report will consist of a Certificate of Attendance rather than a grade awaits a utopia in which all students will learn according to their ability, reveling in the sheer joy of learning.

But, in the meantime, even though the group sampled is quite small, one might consider two possible implications that can be derived from this study of grades and aspirations.

Ability Grouping May Encourage Failure

First: Ability grouping, as an administrative policy, may need to be reviewed. It is not far-fetched to suggest that many students wish to be moved from a higher "track" down to a lower one. Lighter work load, more congenial friends, and other reasons may account for this. Such a movement, it appears, should not be permitted; for if a student perceives any advantage that may be gained from failure, he will fail. If homogeneous groupings are indicated for a school, a final and irrevocable severing of intra-class relationships, by eliminating mobility between tracks, is suggested as the most effective deterrent to students who may be tempted to fail out of one track and into another. For grouping to be successful, we must assume our original placement to be correct, assume changes from track to track to be unnecessary, and where failure occurs, refuse to reward failure with the kind of transfer the student is seeking. Another aspect of ability grouping that might be reviewed is the grading system. To preclude any possibility of grade comparison among tracks, a distinctive grading system for each track is perhaps indicated.

Second: The peculiar construction of the data in the table above implies a direction for further research. This is a most tentative and blurred implication, requiring far more study and thought than has been applied.

Average Students Have Lowest Aspiration Level

It seems uncontestable that a distinctively low-aspiration group emerges from these findings. It is not the low-ability group: Bless them, they'll go through life dreaming of the finest and saying, "Maybe, if only I'd worked a little harder. . . ." And it's not the high-ability group: Their aspirations, if a bit underwhelming, at least tend to concentrate above the average. But how about the middle group: the ordinary student of normal ability who is studying at the usual pace in a regular class? Observe the data: His aspirations are so dulled that, in general, he is content with average or below average grades! Could it be that we who are in education have spent so much time, energy and effort studying the special groups of students with easily identified peculiarities—the slow reader, the musically gifted, the math whiz, the foreign language non-learner, the social studies misfit, the physically handicapped, ad infinitum—that we have missed the gargantuan middle group of the mass of students? Because we have been blind to them as individuals, have we caused a degeneration of aspiration? All is not necessarily well with the masses. We need some research aimed at stimulating the aspirations of the ordinary, average, normal student.

But administrative policy or research study does not implement a solution. The teacher is crucial: he must recognize the problem. And the solution must eventually come through the teacher, if it comes.

In some parts of this and other countries, dog racing is a popular sport. At dog races, a mechanical rabbit runs around the track ahead of the field of dogs. Occasionally one of the racing dogs gets tired of chasing the ordinary mechanical rabbit, and refuses to budge. In such a situation, however, the dog owner does not throw away the dog; he rather searches out a new kind of rabbit—changes its color or size, or gives the dog some other excuse for running. This study suggests that in slum schools our dogs are not chasing our rabbits. Perhaps what we need is a new kind of rabbit!

Useful List of Criteria for Conducting a Critical Analysis of Research Studies

I. The People Involved

- Were the subjects described adequately?
- Who were the subjects in the sample?
- How many? How was the sample chosen?
- What population does the sample represent?

- To what group could conclusions be generalized?
- Were the rights of the subjects violated? (Invasion of privacy/coercion etc.)
- Would the subjects benefit from the research?

II. Purpose of the Research

- What is the purpose of the research?
- Where did the purpose of the research originate?
- What is the specific problem statement?
- Was the purpose or problem clearly stated?
- Who sponsored the research?
- How and by whom were the questions generated?
- What is the relationship of the problem to previous research knowledge?
- Was the argument logical?

III. Methodology

- What research methodology was employed?
- Was the methodology appropriate to the purpose of the problem?
- Were the variables measured? How were the variables measured?
- Was the measurement of the variables adequate?
- Issue of objectivity vs. subjectivity?
- Under what conditions was the research conducted?
- Was the analysis of the data adequate?

IV. Results

- What were the results?
- What can and cannot be concluded from the results?
- How accessible are results? To whom?
- Do the results follow from the methodology?
- Is data, upon which results are based, accessible?
- How will research results be used?
- Were the limitations of the research clearly stated?
- Are conclusions clearly stated?
- Is the need for further research stated or evident?

V. Underlying Assumptions

- Definitions (stated or implied)?
- (learning, education, motivation, development, growth are examples of terms that might be defined in light of a particular study).
- Did you detect any *bias* of the researcher?
- Could researcher bias contaminate the study?
- What assumptions are implicit in the research methodology used?
- What other underlying assumptions are implied in this research study?

Chapter 3

Quasi-Experimental Study— "Head Start" Experience and the Development of Skills and Abilities in Kindergarten Children*2

ELEANOR S. KAPLAN

Critics' Note

> The present article would be classified as an example of educational evaluation. There is disagreement among experts-regarding the distinction between evaluation and research. Some say that the purpose of evaluation is to derive assessments of the worth of particular instances of educational undertakings such as individual textbooks and specific programs; the purpose of research is to produce generalizable conclusions. We see the distinction primarily to be one of purpose rather than procedure. In both studies we ask whether the activities followed permitted the investigator to accomplish the objectives of the study.

* Originally appeared in Graduate Research in Education and Related Disciplines, April 1966, pp.4-28

Introduction

Project Head Start, a federal program under the supervision of the office of Economic Opportunity, was introduced in the summer of 1965. This project was developed as a result of the urgent interest in a national program to prepare economically and socially disadvantaged children for kindergarten. In New York City, more than eighteen thousand young-sters participated in this pre-kindergarten program.

The purpose of this study was to evaluate whether the children who participated in Project Head Start were better prepared for kindergarten than those who did not participate, with particular reference to verbal communication abilities, visual discrimination and naming abilities, and certain motor coordination skills.

There is a strong and growing movement to establish pre-schools of this nature for socially and economically deprived children who are four and five years of age. It is felt that the formation of pre-schools will provide these children with challenge, enrichment, and a desire to learn in school. As a consequence of this type of compensatory program, it is hoped that eventually some of the potential deficiencies resulting from the environment in which these children live, can be overcome.

Compared with children from more privileged environments, chil-dren from marginal social and economic circumstances frequently enter school with poorer preparation for the demands of the learning processes and the behavioral requirements of the classroom. For these children, vital aspects of growing and learning are not provided by the home and must therefore be provided through some other medium such as the school. (Brunner, 1964)

In order to counteract some of the poor effects of a culturally disad-vantaged environment on school performance, it is necessary to provide enrichment and training in the skills and abilities underlying success in the classroom. The pre-kindergarten age of about four or five years is now considered the opportune time to begin striving toward these goals.

Review of the Literature

The concern with the socially and culturally disadvantaged as a specific educational problem is relatively recent. This interest has been fostered by the increasing urbanization of our population and by the awareness of stratification and differential privilege within our society. Riessman (1962) says that cultural deprivation is used interchangeably with educational deprivation to refer to the limited access to education on the part of the lower socioeconomic groups. This is the sense in which the term will be employed in this study. Henry (1963) pointed out that the middle-class home contains a "hidden curriculum" which enables the child to deal appropriately with his first school experience. The disadvantaged home contains no such curriculum and, as pointed out by Deutch (1964, 1965a), is discontinuous with the school environment.

Passow (1963) asserted that the deficiencies of the children from disadvantaged circumstances can be overcome by proper educational planning. He emphasized the importance of early compensation for the deficiencies in the home environment. Riessman (1962) argued, however, that educational programs for the disadvantaged can begin at any age. Such programs, according to Riessman (1964) should consider the strengths that disadvantaged children possess in nonverbal communication and independence, and that they should not rely on the middle-class model. However, Riessman's argument on cultural relativism does not take into consideration the increasing industrialization of our society and the greater dependence in such a society on verbal conmunication, which entails the need for facility in verbal skills such as reading and writing.

John (1963) examined certain patterns of linguistic and cognitive behavior in examples of Negro children and reported that consistent class differences in language skills were shown to emerge between groups of Negro children of different socio-economic classes. Middle-class children from more advantaged environments were reported to have a better command of language in terms of its classificatory and problem-solving functions. Middle-class Negro children surpassed their lower-class age mates in possessing a larger vocabulary (WISC Vocabulary results) and a higher non-verbal intelligence quotient (Lorge-Thorndike IQ Test) in their ability to produce a best-fit response. The middle-class child had an advantage over the lower-class child in tasks requiring precise and somewhat abstract language due to the amount of help available to him in his home. The acquisition of more abstract and integrative language seemed to be hampered by the living conditions in the homes of the lower-class children.

The educational implications of these findings point to the need for greater emphasis on language teaching for disadvantaged children. In studying different verbal learning tasks, Jensen (1963) found that paired-associate learning involved greater reliance on verbal mediations than did serial learning. According to John (1963) and Bernstein (1960,

1962), the socially disadvantaged were less facile in the use of verbal mediators. The above studies elucidate the educational problem involved in attempting to reverse the effects of environmental linguistic deprivation. (Kendler, 1963)

According to the formulation of Bernstein (1960), the cumulative deficiency in language functioning results from the failure in development through the years of an elaborated language system with accurate grammatical order and logical modifiers, mediated through a grammatically complex sentence structure, containing prepositions, impersonal pronouns, and a discriminative selection of adjectives and adverbs. Bernstein (1960) asserts that lower-class speech is characterized by simple, unfinished sentences and a rigid, limited use of adjectives and adverbs. He also evaluated the complexity of sentences (simple or complex) and the percentage of adjectives and adverbs of the total words spoken by the subjects during the verbal part of the test. The usage of adjectives and adverbs is the start of a more complex type of verbal communication. Two related studies (C.P. Deutsch, 1964; John & Goldstein, 1964) indicated that lower-class deprived homes are deficient in the stimulation required for adequate development of discrimination and of language skills.

Montague (1964) tested kindergarten children on arithmetic concepts and showed that those from high socio-economic areas scored significantly higher on the inventory than those from low socio-economic areas. This tends to confirm the view of Deutsch (1962,p.8) that:

> A child from any circumstance who has been deprived of a substantial portion of the variety of stimuli which he is maturationally capable of responding to is likely to be deficient in both the formal and contentual equipment required for learning.

The major emphasis in educational programming for disadvantaged children has been to initiate programs before the gap between these children and their more advantaged peers widens beyond reach. This emphasis has led to the development of programs on the nursery or pre-school level. Nursery schools have been expanding since the beginning of the twentieth century. There were three nursery schools in the United States in 1918 and by 1931 the number had grown to five hundred. Private nursery schools and experimental schools connected to universities have been popular with the more privileged groups. Nursery schools for the poor were encouraged and financially supported by the federal government during the depression under President Franklin Delano Roosevelt. In 1933, some 2,400 nursery school programs were in operation in the United States, most of them supported by the WPA. During World War II the federal government put its support behind nursery schools, known then as Child Care Centers, where working mothers could leave their preschool-age children. In the past few years a great emphasis has been placed on preschool education for the culturally deprived.

The usefulness of preschool programs that are oriented toward the stimulation of cognitive development found general support in Fowler (1962) and in Jensen(1963). The psychological basis for such programs was specifically elaborated by Hunt (1964) and their usefulness explicitly upheld by Deutch (1964b). Hunt (1964) examined evidence which refuted the concepts of fixed intelligence and predetermined development. It is experience, he argued, particularly experience that comes before the advent of language, that is important. He regards the effects of cultural deprivation in infancy and early childhood. He indicated that appropriately organized cognitive stimulation during the preschool years can be highly effective in accelerating the development of intellectual functions. He recommended a curriculum that is consistent with children's environmental experience and their initial abilities and disabilities. Hunt (1964) also cited evidence in support of programs for preschool enrichment for culturally deprived children and asserted that such children are poorly prepared to meet the demands of the school and that initial failures are almost inevitable. Hunt assumed that the culture of the lower-class environment is different from the culture that has molded the school and its educational theory and this idea is also supported by Riessman (1962).

Deutsch (1965a) felt that the goal of a preschool program for disadvantaged children should be:

> . . . to stimulate in young children the skills that underlie school performance and which according to both research findings and practical school experience are evidently not stimulated by disadvantaged backgrounds and poor environments. A broader goal is to help each child to realize more fully his own productive potential for his own good and for the good of society. (p.51)

Current preschool programs for the culturally disadvantaged proceed on the assumption that the deprived child's academic deficit increases as he moves through the grades. (Stine,1965) An early school program is needed to head off the cumulative deficiency and to attempt to neutralize cultural deprivation before school entrance. The early school admission of children from depressed areas should specifically aid language development and abstract thinking. It should provide a pleasurable emotional experience and new opportunity for the development of social and intellectual ability. (Stine, 1965) However, it is generally recognized that early intervention by the school is not likely to succeed if it is not accompanied by reinforcement and support in the home. Parents should be brought into such programs at the beginning as partners in the educational enterprise. Their resources for serving in this capacity are much greater than is generally realized. (Haskell, 1965)

Spurred by Ford Foundation grants and the Johnson Administration's War on Poverty, preschool education programs for culturally deprived children are moving along on a state-wide basis in Pennsylvania, as well as in four eastern cities, New York, New Haven, Baltimore and Boston. Each program is developing its own methods of introducing educationally underprivileged children to experiences and thinking patterns that will help them start school on a par with other students. Although the goals of the plans are similar, each program has developed in its own way. Similar preschool projects for culturally deprived children are currently underway in many cities throughout the nation but progress reports are not yet available.

Project Head Start was introduced in the summer of 1965 on an experimental basis by the U.S. Office of Economic Opportunity to provide preschool learning experiences for deprived children who otherwise would not be exposed to such benefits. The program has already benefited some 560,000 youngsters in 2,500 communities in the United States. Reference can be made to only a few of the many Head Start centers as there are only thirty-five children in this study.

There have been various criticisms made about the Head Start Project: the program was very expensive (it cost about $112,000,000) and it was insufficiently prepared and rushed through. There was inadequate provision for evaluation and follow-up. Many experts have complained that Head Start lacked the kind of experimental preparation such as pre-testing and careful study of the selected population. Thus far, the official reports are only based on a small sample of the children in certain centers and are unscientific and sketchy. (Hechinger, 1965b) In addition, there were no criteria established to judge the effectiveness or preparedness of the teachers in the project. Deutsch (Hechinger, 1965b) said that many of the programs lacked the necessary preparedness and certain others were purely custodial. It has been pointed out that compensatory education for children of deprived minorities is no substitute for changes in the structure of education itself. (Hechinger, 1965; Riessman, 1962) It is of little use to give minority group children an opportunity to begin slightly ahead of the class, if, at the same time, their regular schooling is not made relevant to them. The school itself must continue to develop the parent participation fostered in Head Start. (Hechinger, 1965a)

Prior educational research has shown that early compensatory education is of very limited, short-term benefit-unless there is a consistent follow-up. If children's gains are not constantly reinforced through the years, they disappear within a few years. Dr. Edmund W. Gordon, Head Start's director of research said: "It is vital that the summer crash program not be regarded as a substitute for the regular and continuing education of disadvantaged children." (Hechinger,1965b, p.75) An inherent danger of the project is that it may deceive the public into believing that early success can be easily translated into later success without the investment of money, time, and personnel on a continuous basis. This painful lesson has been demonstrated by the initial success but long-term failure of New York City's Higher Horizons Program. (Hechinger, 1965b)

Although it is too early to evaluate the long-term success of the preschool programs for disadvantaged children because they are very recent undertakings, some of the immediate effects can be evaluated. Gang, a principal of a Harlem elementary school has, for instance, reported that many teachers in his school have found better school adjustment among the Head Start children as compared to children who did not participate in the program. (Hechinger, 1965b)

Project Head Start has received the approval of the United Parents Association in New York City. Although it cautioned against making premature educational judgments about the Head Start program, the UPA commended the break-through made in reaching the hitherto hard-to-reach parents of disadvantaged children. The UPA, through its visits to the child centers, found that although the staff of teachers, aides, and volunteers was adequate, some of the physical plants were not. A report issued to the New York City Board of Education by the UPA recommended more adequate planning for future preschool projects, establishment of a liaison between the winter and summer staff, and smaller classes in all early childhood programs. (Emery,1965)

One of the main goals of Project Head Start was to develop speech and verbal communication through "show and tell," listening to sounds, discrimination between sounds, using names to individuate, and listening to records and tape recordings. (Graham & Hess, 1965) For the purposes of this investigation, verbal communication will be operationally defined in this study as verbal fluency, enunciation, verbal usage, verbal ability to structure sentences, and story-telling ability.

A second goal was to develop the visual and observational abilities of the children by having them become familiar with the letters of the alphabet, classify objects, become aware of the environment, combine awareness of environment with learning similarities and differences, reading pictures, and distinguishing colors and shapes. (Graham & Hess, 1965) Visual discrimination and naming abilities will be operationally defined as ability to discriminate and name various colors and shapes. Demonstrations were used in Head Start to help teach the motor coordination skills such as buttoning, cutting, and coloring with crayons. (Graham & Hess, 1965) Throughout this study, motor coordination skills were interpreted as skill in cutting, buttoning one's clothes, coloring and drawing the figure of a man. Other goals of the Head Start program were to develop a sense of self, develop creativity, self-expression, and curiosity through science.

The present study was designed to compare children who had participated in Project Head Start with children who had not participated in the project in order to assess the immediate benefits of this experience.

Hypotheses

Kindergarten children who participated in Project Head Start will be superior to a matched group of children who did not participate in Project Head Start in:

1. Verbal communication abilities, as measured by:
   a) verbal fluency
   b) enunciation
   c) ability to structure sentences
   d) story-telling ability
   e) verbal usage.

2. Visual discrimination and naming abilities, as measured by:
   a) naming colors
   b) naming of shapes

3. Motor coordination skills, as measured by:
   a) drawing figures
   b) coloring
   c) cutting
   d) buttoning their clothing.

Procedure

This study was conducted in a public elementary school in a lower-class neighborhood. The school provides special services such as additional reading teachers, guidance counselors, non-English coordinators, and instructional materials designed to accelerate the achievement of children of low socio-economic background who are limited in their development by environmental factors beyond their control.

Sample

The subjects selected for this study were seventy disadvantaged kindergarten children between the ages of four years eight months and five years six months. The experimental group consisted of thirty-five children who had participated in Project Head Start during the previous summer. The control group consisted of thirty-five children with no preschool experience.

Individual children in the control group and the experimental group were matched on the following criteria:

1. **Sex**: Each pair consisted of two members of the same sex. There were fourteen girls and twenty-one boys in each group.
2. **Ethnic Background**: Each pair consisted of two members of the same race. There were seventeen Negro and eighteen Puerto Rican children in each group.
3. **Age**: The maximum difference in ages for the members of a pair was four months.
4. **Language in the home**: Each pair consisted of two members in whose homes the same languages were spoken.

5. **Age of siblings**: The ages of the siblings of the matched pairs were similar.

The socio-economic status of the families of the subjects was approximately the same . It was assumed that the factors of sex, ethnic background, age, language spoken in the home, and age of siblings provided an accurate method of matching the two groups of kindergarten children in this study.

Techniques of Measurement

A "Describe This Picture Test" was designed by the researcher to determine verbal communication abilities. The test, which was given to each child individually, consisted of a picture of two firetrucks going to a fire, two police stopping traffic, people watching, and a dog running behind the trucks. The children were asked to: "Tell me everything that you see in this picture." Subsequently, each subject was told: "Tell me a story about this picture." Testing was stopped when each subject insisted that he had nothing more to say.

The subjects were graded on their verbal abilities in terms of their ability to tell a story, ability to structure sentences, verbal fluency, verbal usage, and enunciation. Ability to tell a story was rated according to the complexity of statements about the picture. For purposes of computation a numerical value of zero was assigned if nothing was said; a value of one was assigned if the picture was described; a value of two was assigned if the picture was described with considerable detail; a value of three was assigned if an organized story was told; a value of four was assigned if an organized creative story was told.

The ability of the subjects to structure sentences was rated as follows: a value of zero was assigned if nothing was said; a value of one if phrases were used; a value of two if the subject used simple sentences, a value of three if the subject used complex sentences.

Verbal fluency was measured by the total number of words employed in describing and telling a story about the picture. The verbal usage score was the percentage of adjectives and adverbs of the total number of words used by the subject.

The enunciation ability of the subject was rated by assigning a score of one to enunciation which was fairly clear and a score of two to enunciation which was very clear.

Specific instruments devised by the investigator were used to measure certain visual discrimination and naming abilities which had been developed in the Project Head Start. Each subject was given an individual oral test to measure his grasp of color concepts. This test consisted of showing each child four shapes colored red, blue, yellow, and green and then asking the child to name each color. One point was given for each color named correctly.

Three of these shapes were used again in a similar procedure to test the subjects' ability to identify the shapes of a circle, a square, and a triangle. If the child named some object that resembled the shape, the child's exact words were recorded. One point was given for each shape named correctly and one-half point was given for each object similar to the shape named, if the name of shape was not stated.

In order to evaluate motor coordination skills each child was asked to draw a picture of a man, and it was rated using norms set up in the Good-enough-Draw-A-Man Test for Negro Elementary School children. This rating scale was used as a measure of drawing skill and not as a measure of intelligence, as it is commonly used. The possibility that intelligence quotients were raised by participation in Project Head Start was not evaluated in this study.

In order to test cutting and coloring skills, subjects were each given a simple outline of a squirrel and told to color and cut it out with a scissors. The subjects had previously seen pictures of squirrels and had discussed them. The completed productions were rated according to how well the child was able to follow the squirrel outline in cutting and also the type of stroke used in coloring with crayons. The rating scale for both skills was as follows: poor was assigned a numerical value of one; fair a value of two; good a value of three; very good a value of four; excellent a value of five.

An observational technique was used to evaluate the subjects' ability to button their own coats or sweaters. Every day before the children left school they lined up before the investigator who observed which children were able to button their own clothing and which children could not perform this task. Those who stated that they could not button their own clothing were urged to try in order to eliminate the possibility that they merely desired the adult's attention. A score of one was given if the subject was able to button his own coat and a score of zero was given if he could not.

Former Project Head Start students were identified from their cumulative record cards. The admission forms of all the students provided information on sex, date of birth, race, age, number of siblings, and languages spoken in the home. These data were used to match the students. All of the instruments designed to test the visual discrimination abilities and motor coordination skills were presented to the children at the beginning of kindergarten in order to insure that these skills and abilities to be tested were not learned during the kindergarten experience.

Both verbal communication ability tests and visual discrimination ability tests were presented to each subject individually in a quiet room where a table and two chairs had previously been arranged. Each subject was allowed as much time as he needed to answer each question and was reminded of the directions at short intervals. He was permitted to change his mind (if he wanted to) and was asked to guess if he was unsure. The subject was not told whether he was right or wrong but was encouraged throughout the testing procedure. After each question was answered, he was told that he had done very well.

The children's performance was evaluated, according to specific criteria, by the investigator and an additional rater who had also been working with these subjects. The investigator had done the original classification of the experimental and control groups, but made no effort to remember who was in each group during the study. The other rater had no knowledge at any time of the names of the subjects in each classification. Each scorer worked independently without knowledge of the scores assigned by the other. The results showed very close rater agreement. In the few instances where larger differences occurred, each rater reevaluated his scoring individually. One limitation of this study was that the researcher may have been unconsciously aware of the group classification of some of the children and this may have influenced some of the scoring of the skills and abilities of the subjects.

A second limitation of this study was that it was not possible to test the children in the skills and abilities investigated herein prior to their attendance in Project Head Start. It is possible that the two groups differed on the various abilities before the Head Start program began.

Analysis of the Data

The median score on each test was obtained for each group and used to compare the performance of the two groups. The over-all median of each test was obtained from the combined test scores of all seventy subjects in order to dichotomize the groups on test performance. Eleven chi-square tests using these medians were performed and the .05 level of significance chosen as the critical value.

Critics' Note

For each set of data the investigator conducted a chi-square test of the statistical significance of the difference between the score distribution found for the two groups of children. The investigator was seeking to determine whether the difference in proportion of students in the two groups who are above a particular score could happen by chance alone. Specifically, the statistical test indicates the probability of getting such a large difference in proportions if only chance (i.e., sampling variability) were operating. When this probability is small (defined in this paper as less than 5%) and thus the chance-alone hypotheses is not very plausible, the investigator indicates that the difference was statistically significant and presumably, the Head Start program had an effect.

Results

Verbal Communication Abilities

It was hypothesized that kindergarten children who participated in Project Head Start would be superior in the following verbal communication abilities: (a) ability in telling a story; (b) ability to structure sentences; (c) verbal fluency; (d) verbal usage; (e) enunciation.

Table 3.1 shows the story-telling ratings for children in the Head Start and non-Head Start groups. The median rating for the Head Start group was 3.3 and for the non-Head Start group 2.3. The median for the combined group was 2.8. Using 3 and above as the upper category, the chi-square median test ($x^2 = 5.74$) was statistically significant (p .025), indicating that the children in the Head Start group showed greater ability in telling a story.

Table 3.2 presents the ratings of the students' ability to structure sentences. The median of the Head Start group was 3.2 compared to 2.5 for the non-Head Start group. The median for the combined groups was

Table 3.1
Verbal Ability: Telling a Story

	Number of Children Receiving Each Rating	
Story-telling Rating	Head Start (35)	Non-Head Start (35)
4	10	4
3	11	7
2	6	10
1	7	11
0	1	3
	Median = 3.3	Median = 2.3

Table 3.2
Ability to Structure Sentences

	Number of Children Receiving Each Rating	
Scale Rating for Sentence Structure Used	Head Start (35)	Non-Head Start (35)
3	22	11
2	9	14
1	3	5
0	1	5
	Median = 3.2	Median = 2.5

2.9. Using 3 as the upper category, the chi-square median test in effect compared children who gave complex sentences with those who did not. The chi-square value of 6.94 was statistically significant (p .01). The Head Start group thus excelled the non-Head Start group in the ability to speak in complex sentences.

Table 3.3 presents the results of the verbal fluency test. The number of words used by the subjects on the "Describe This Picture" test ranged from 0 through 270. The median of the Head Start group was 96 and the non-Head Start group median was 74. The median for the combined group was 86. The chi-square median test ($x^2 = 4.64$) was statistically significant (p .05), indicating that the Head Start group was superior in verbal fluency to the non Head-Start group.

Table 3.3
Verbal Fluency

Number of Words Used	Number of Children Using Indicated Number of Words	
	Head Start (35)	Non-Head Start (35)
241-270	1	
211-240		2
181-210		1
151-180	5	
121-150	3	4
91-120	10	6
61-90	10	8
31-60	5	8
0-30	1	6
	Median = 96	Median = 74

Table 3.4
Verbal Usage

Percentage of Adjectives and Adverbs	Number of Children Giving Indicated Percentage	
	Head Start (35)	Non-Head Start (35)
24, 26%	1	
21-23		
18-20		1
15-17		
12-14	3	4
9-11	10	7
6-8	8	1
3-5	8	11
0-2	5	11
	Median = 7.7%	Median = 4.8%

The distribution of scores received by subjects in verbal usage is shown in Table 3.4 and is expressed as the percentage of total words which were adjectives and adverbs. The percentages ranged from 0 through 26%. The median was 7.7% for the Head Start group as compared with 4.8% for the non-Head Start group. The obtained chi-square value (4.64) was statistically significant (p .05), indicating that the Head Start group used more adjectives and adverbs in their speech.

To evaluate the child's enunciation, a rating of 1 or 2 was assigned according to the clarity of speech of the subjects on the "Describe This Picture" test. Table 3.5 gives the distributions of ratings for the two groups. The chi-square 2 value obtained from the enunciation ratings ($x^2 = 2.81$) was not statistically significant (.05 p .10).

Critics' Note

The parenthetical expression given directly above should have been written: (.05 p .10). The symbol, " $<$ " means "less than." Thus, the probability of differences between two groups on enunciation scores as large as those actually found could be expected to occur 5 to 10 percent of the time, even if chance alone were operating (i.e., program had no effect). This probability was not small enough for the investigator to reject with confidence the hypothesis that for a population of children similar to these 70, no differences on this variable would be found.

The chi-square values for verbal story-telling ability, ability to structure sentences, verbal fluency, and verbal usage were all statistically significant at less than the .05 level. The chi-square value for the enunciation rating was not statistically significant. The hypothesis that kindergarten students who participated in Project Head Start are superior in specific verbal abilities was supported except for enunciation ability.

Visual Discrimination and Naming Abilities

It was hypothesized that kindergarten children who participated in Project Head Start would be superior to non-Head Start children in naming colors and in naming shapes.

Table 3.5
Enunciation Ratings

Clarity of Speech Rating	Number of Children Receiving Rating	
	Head Start (35)	Non-Head Start (35)
2	22	15
1	13	20

Table 3.6
Naming Colors

Number of Colors Named Correctly	Number of Children with Indicated Score	
	Head Start (35)	Non-Head Start (35)
4	20	8
3	2	4
2	5	7
1	7	10
0	1	0
	Median = 4.0	Median = 2.2

Table 3.6 presents the data obtained on the naming colors test. The range of possible colors which could be correctly identified was from 0 through 4, with one point given for each color named correctly. The median for the Head Start group was 4.0 compared to 2.2 for the non Head Start group. The chi-square median test ($x^2 = 5.72$) was statistically significant (p .025), indicating that the Head Start group was superior in the visual discrimination ability of naming colors.

Table 3.7 presents data showing subjects' ability to name shapes. The possible range of scores for shapes named correctly was from 0 through 3 including half points for objects named that are similar to the shapes. A median of 2.1 was obtained by the Head Start group and a median of 1.4 by the non-Head Start group. The chi-square median test ($x^2 = 5.72$) was statically significant (p .025), indicating that Head Start children were superior in naming shapes.

Table 3.7
Naming Shapes

Number of Shapes Named Correctly	Number of Children with Indicated Score	
	Head start (35)	Non-Head Start (35)
3.0	0	3
2.5		
2.0	11	9
1.5	3	1
1.0	10	13
.5		
0	2	9
	Median = 2.1	Median = 1.4

The chi-square values obtained for naming colors and naming shapes were statistically significant. The hypothesis that kindergarten students who participated in Project Head Start are superior in visual discrimination as measured by the ability to name correctly colors and shapes was supported by this data.

Table 3.8
Drawing Skill

Score on Figure Drawing Task	Number of Children with Indicated Score	
	Head Start (35)	Non-Head Start (35)
50-59	1	
40-49		
30-39	8	2
20-29	12	10
10-19	11	14
0-9	3	9
	Median = 23	Median = 16

Motor Coordination Skills

The third hypothesis was that kindergarten children who participated in Project Head Start would be superior to non-Head Start children in the specific motor coordination skills of drawing, coloring, cutting, and buttoning one's clothing.

The results of the drawing task are presented in Table 3.8. The elements which appeared in the children's drawings were rated according to a scale set up by Goodenough (Kennedy and Lindner, 1964). The scores ranged from 0 through 59. A median of 23 was obtained for the Head Start group, compared to a median of 16 for the non-Head Start group. The chi-square median test (x^2 = 4.64 was statistically significant (p .05). The Head Start group was thus superior in their drawing ability.

Table 3.9
Coloring Skill

Score on Coloring Task	Number of Children with Indicated Score	
	Head Start (35)	Non-Head Start (35)
5	16	8
4	6	2
3	3	3
2	2	5
1	8	17
	Median = 4.8	Median = 2.1

Table 3.9 presents the results of the coloring task. The scores had a possible range from 1 (poor) through 5 (excellent). The median was 4.8 for the Head Start group and 2.1 for the non-Head Start group. The chi-square median test 2 (x^2 = 8.28) was statistically significant (p .005). The Head Start group thus showed superior skill on the coloring task.

Table 3.10
Cutting Skill

	Number of Children with Indicated Score	
Score on Cutting Task	Head Start (35)	Non-Head Start (35)
5	16	8
4	5	5
3	5	8
2	4	7
1	5	7
	Median = 4.7	Median = 3.4

Table 3.10 presents the data on the cutting task. The possible range of scores was from 1 (poor) through 5 (excellent). The Head Start median was 4.7 and the non-Head Start median was 3.4. A chi-square median test was performed and the obtained value of 3.66 is slightly less than the value of 3.84 needed for significance at the .05 level. Thus, the hypothesis that the Head Start group is superior to the non-Head Start group in cutting skill could not be supported.

Table 3.11
Buttoning Skill

	Number of Children with Indicated Score	
Rating	Head Start (35)	Non-Head-Start (35)
1	28	12
0	7	23

The results of observing buttoning skill are shown in Table 3.11. The subjects were given a rating of 1 if they could button their clothing by themselves and 0 if they could not. The chi-square test ($x^2 = 14.94$) was statistically significant (p .001). The Head Start group thus showed superior motor coordination skill in the ability to button their clothing by themselves.

The chi-square values for motor coordination skill tests of drawing, coloring, and buttoning of clothing were statistically significant at less than the .05 level. Only cutting skill resulted in a chi-square which was not statistically significent although the results were in the predicted direction. The hypothesis that kindergarten children who participated in Project Head Start are superior in certain motor coordination skills was thus generally supported by the results.

Discussion

It was predicted that kindergarten children who had participated in Project Head Start would be superior to children who had no preschool experience in specific verbal abilities, visual discrimination and naming abilities, and motor coordination skills. The rationale behind this prediction was that the stated goals of the Head Start program indicated the development of these skills and abilities.

The results of this study indicate that kindergarten children who had attended the Head Start program were superior to those who had not in each of the skills and abilities tested. These results agree with the views of others who consider the preschool participation an enriching and valuable experience for the culturally deprived child.

The major speech pattern of the lower classes (Bernstein, 1960) is characterized by grammatically simple and often unfinished sentences, poor syntactical form, simple and repetitive use of conjunctions, and a rigid, limited use of adjectives and adverbs. The findings of this study regarding verbal abilities indicate that children participating in the Head Start program showed greater story-telling ability, especially in telling creative, organized stories than non-participants. They were also superior in the type of sentences employed, including the use of complex sentences. In addition the Head Start participants possessed greater verbal fluency and used a greater percentage of adjectives and adverbs. They did not, however, show greater clarity in their speech than the non-Head Start group. It appears though, that the Head Start children gained in their ability to communicate verbally. Bernstein (1960) also stated that the discriminative selection of adjectives and adverbs and the use of accurate grammatical order and complex sentence structure give direction to the organization of thinking. It is therefore likely that since the Head Start children were found to be more adept verbally, they may also be more capable of handling standard intellectual and linguistic tasks.

The results showed that the subjects in the Head Start program performed better on three of the four tests for motor coordination skill. The

Head Start children were superior in drawing the figure of a man. According to Goodenough, Anastasi and D'Angelo (1952), and Anastasi and DeJesus (1953), the ability to draw a man is related to intelligence. The data indicated that the Head Start children were also superior in coloring and buttoning their clothing. Although the Head Start children also tended to do better in cutting skills, the results did not reach statistical significance.

The Head Start group was superior in visual discrimination and naming of colors and shapes. The development of these discrimination abilities is related to learning how to read which, in turn, is the basic skill needed for a successful educational experience.

In a paper by John (1965) reporting on work done at the Institute for Developmental Studies in New York, it was suggested that the middle-class child has an advantage over the lower-class child because of the tutoring available to him in his home. She emphasized that without such help it is very difficult for a child to acquire the more abstract and precise use of language. The Head Start enrichment experience may serve as a supplement to or a substitute for the home and help to develop the necessary skills and abilities early in the life of the child.

It may be that an effective enrichment program, introduced at the earliest possible time in the child's life, would prevent the cumulative deficit cited by Bernstein (1960) and Deutsch (1965b). As the child develops, it becomes progressively more difficult to reverse this deficit which increases through the years. Although some of the cumulative deficiency is associated with inadequate early preparation due to environmental deficiencies, the inadequacy of the school environment is also suggested by the researcher as a contributing cause.

The deficiencies which the home environment, inadequate educational facilities and other factors have helped to create for the culturally deprived child cannot be expected to be modified or eliminated during a summer or even in a year's enrichment program. The child's deprivation may be too deeply ingrained to be overcome in preschool and therefore this type of program should be continued throughout the early elementary grades to provide a continuity of enrichment experiences for these children. Otherwise, the results which are achieved in the preschool experience may disappear through the years as a result of crowded classrooms, inappropriate curriculum (Riessman, 1962), and other educational handicaps.

Future research should concern itself with continued examination of the values of the preschool program. These studies should be longitudinal and examine students prior, during, and for a number of years after participation in the program in order to assess the long-range benefits of the preschool program. It is vital to the success of the preschool program that the learning experiences needed to overcome the effects of the environmental limitations on children from deprived backgrounds are identified. More experimentation and exploration in this area of curriculum development for the culturally deprived child is necessary.

The experiences provided in the instructional program made it possible for children in the preschool Head Start project to become more adept in certain verbal abilities, visual discrimination abilities, and motor coordination skills. Longitudinal studies would be valuable in determining whether Head Start participants will be better school achievers than their non-Head Start counterparts as they progress in school.

Summary

The purpose of this study was to assess whether the children who participated in Project Head Start were better prepared for kindergarten than those who did not participate in regard to verbal communication, visual discrimination and naming, and motor coordination skills. It was hypothesized that kindergarten children who participated in Project Head Start would be superior in verbal communication abilities as measured by verbal fluency, verbal usage, enunciation, ability to structure sentences, and ability to tell a story; that they would be superior in the visual discrimination and naming of colors and shapes; and that they would be superior in motor coordination skill, as measured by drawing figures, coloring, cutting, and buttoning their clothing.

The subjects were seventy kindergarten children between the ages of four and five who were identified on the basis of whether or not they had participated in the Head Start program during the summer of 1965. Thirty-five children who had participated in this project were paired with thirty-five children who had not participated in the project using sex, age, ethnic background, language spoken in the home, age of siblings, and preschool experience as the criteria.

The subjects were then compared with respect to their verbal communication abilities. They were asked to tell everything they saw in a sample picture and to tell a story about that picture. They were rated according to the ability to structure sentences, story-telling ability, verbal fluency, verbal usage, and enunciation.

The subjects in each group were also compared in their visual discrimination abilities. Four colors and three shapes were presented to each child who was then asked to name each color and shape. The children's productions provided data to evaluate their cutting, coloring, and drawing skills. The children's ability to button their own clothing was also observed.

The data were analyzed in terms of a comparison between the Head Start and non-Head Start groups, utilizing chi-square median tests of significance. The Head Start group did significantly better than the non-Head Start group in all hypothesized abilities and skills except for enunciation ability and cutting skill which did not reach statistical significance.

The present findings support the current view that culturally deprived children benefit from preschool enrichment programs. It was suggested that future research should further examine the values of preschool compensatory programs and establish an appropriate curriculum. Longitudinal studies are needed in order to ascertain the long-term benefits of such a program.

Useful List of Criteria for Conducting a Critical Analysis of Research Studies

I. The People Involved

- Were the subjects described adequately?
- Who were the subjects in the sample? How many?
- How was the sample chosen?
- What population does the sample represent?
- To what group could conclusions be generalized?
- Were the rights of the subjects violated? (Invasion of privacy/coercion etc.)
- Would the subjects benefit from the research?

II. Purpose of the Research

- What is the purpose of the research?
- Where did the purpose of the research originate?
- What is the specific problem statement?
- Was the purpose or problem clearly stated?
- Who sponsored the research?
- How and by whom were the questions generated?
- What is the relationship of the problem to previous research knowledge?
- Was the argument logical?

III. Methodology

- What research methodology was employed?
- Was the methodology appropriate to the purpose of the problem?
- Were the variables measured? How were the variables measured?
- Was the measurement of the variables adequate?
- Issue of objectivity vs. subjectivity?
- Under what conditions was the research conducted?
- Was the analysis of the data adequate?

IV. Results

- What were the results?
- What can and cannot be concluded from the results?
- How accessible are results? By whom?
- Do the results follow from the methodology?
- Is data, upon which results are based, accessible?
- How will research results be used?
- Were the limitations of the research clearly stated?
- Are conclusions clearly stated?
- Is the need for further research stated or evident?

V. Underlying Assumptions

- Definitions (stated or implied)?
- (learning, education, motivation, development, growth are examples of terms that might be defined in light of a particular study).
- Did you detect any *bias* of the researcher?
- Could researcher bias contaminate the study?
- What assumptions are implicit in the research methodology used?
- What other underlying assumptions are implied in this research study?

Note

1. This study was carried out under the supervision of Judith Greenberg and David J. Fox

Chapter 4

An Introduction to Qualitative/Ethnographic Research

Over the past decade, there has been growing interest in the subjective, in meaning, and in common sense understandings. This interest has been accompanied by changes in the way we conduct research. The questionnaire, the formal interview, and the laboratory experiment, though still important, are no longer as dominant as they once were. They are methods that are used by those seeking objective answers based on a quantitative methodology.

In research, the term methodology in a broad sense, refers to the process, principle and procedures by which we approach problems and seek answers. In the social sciences, the term applies to how one conducts research. As in everything we do, our assumptions, interests, and goals greatly influence which methodological procedures we choose. When reduced to their essentials, most debates over methods are debates over assumptions and goals, over theory and perspective.

Two major theoretical perspectives have dominated the social science and research scene. The positivists hold one view and the phenomenologists take another view. The positivists and the phenomenologists approach different problems and seek different answers. Their research will typically demand different methodologies.

Qualitative methodologies refer to research procedures which produce descriptive data: written or spoken words and observable behavior.

Qualitative methodology is, in effect—"fieldwork." In effect, you go into the field of interest and "discover categories" of meaning that "emerge." The nightmare of a person involved in qualitative or field-work methodology is, "What do I do if I don't find anything?" A double life is often required of the fieldworker who is involved as a participant in whatever little world is under study while, at the same time, attempting to record and make sense out of that world as an observer. The intellectual effort must be high and continuous in this type of research. It is scary because the research outcomes are unpredictable. The emphasis in qualitative research is on discovery as well as verification. In quantitative research, the process of replication and verification is a routine, precisely specified procedure. Hypothesis testing has known and predictable outcomes. Statistics and computer science help one in that type of research.

Participant observation is a useful tool for gathering evidence about processes, circumstances, or other observable conditions. It also helps answer questions like: "How are things happening? What things are happening that we don't usually measure? Under what conditions are they happening? Why are they happening? For example, the quality of education can be influenced by HOW people are teaching (e.g., the infamous hidden curriculum in which schools affect students—to be passive, dull, rather than independent, etc.) or the physical condition of the school, neighborhood, and home. The picture of a school program may be incomplete without such factors (aside from test scores, and curricular options). By watching and probing—valuable information about crucial things that often go unrecorded—can be obtained. (E.g. one might study the relationship between what schools teach and how they teach, one way of measuring problem-solving skills is by seeing if kids can answer a predetermined set of questions correctly. Another way that measures the process of learning and teaching is to observe classes to find out whether teachers are encouraging "scientific" thinking and active learning.)

One should use both approaches. Whenever you investigate school problems, you should experience the school. Asking questions about processes and conditions will tell you a lot about what is happening, how it's happening, and why it's happening. If you investigate using participant observation:

1. Get a flavor of as much of the system as possible.
2. Identify most problems or parts of the system that influence the situation under investigation.

3. Select the problems or parts which seem most important and might provide vital evidence.

For example, extensive school visits—

A. Go through a day as the student does, include time blocks, spaces, halls, yards, etc., before and after school.
B. Which problems occur in which parts of the system. Is it discipline in the principal's office, grading in the classroom, advisement in guidance?
C. Select problems of greatest concern—reduce them to manageable proportions so that your purposes are clear.

Participant observers record facts and put them together into a meaningful picture. As you observe a situation, don't try to memorize it. Simply be aware. To the extent possible, block out emotions and logic—be a sensing device.

After an observation, make notes about what happened. Five types of data are important to the observer:

1. Descriptive data about seeings (physical impressions.)
2. Descriptions of actions and behaviors.
3. Word for word statements.
4. Unobtrusive data—past behavior, clues, if large numbers of cigarette butts in a room may indicate frequent use and/or infrequent cleaning. Offensive graffiti may indicate low student morale.
5. Documents—written material, Ex: census data/student handbooks.

Self Training Exercise

1. Mini observation—15 minute visit
   (record data afterward).
   Purpose: awareness of the observable and what is significant may come later in the study.
2. Conversation—attempt to memorize the key parts of
   a conversation.
   Purpose: helps one to "tune in" on a conversation.

3. Memory Tests—tune in on 10 minute segments of other people's conversations. (Who said what to whom and what sequence.)
4. Community Observations—observe street scenes and actors. *Purpose*: What are people like, etc.
5. Do mock informant interviews.

The procedures outlined above will give you a feeling about what participant observation entails and will enable you to try a pilot study of your own, or perhaps arouse your reading interest in qualitative research in general and participant observation in particular. We have included a participant observation study in the text so that you can appraise an actual qualitative research study.

Personal documents, while not used as frequently as other qualitative research techniques, are used to collect data and are considered to be "subject produced" data. Such things as autobiographies, personal letters, diaries, memos, minutes from meetings, yearbooks, scrapbooks, personnel files, and students' case records and folders are often included under the category of data appropriate in a qualitative study. Personal document refers to any first-person narrative produced by an individual which describes the person's own actions, experiences, and beliefs. Written material becomes personal in this framework when it is self-revealing of the person's view of experiences. The transcripts of interviews could be considered a personal document, but in the sense of "personal document" used in this discussion, it refers only to materials that have been written by the subjects themselves. Personal document qualitative research seeks "to discover" those already written materials. Official documents with their often "official perspective" are also sought after by the qualitative researcher who wishes to gather whatever data leads to an "understanding" of the person or subject in the "context" of how it sees others and is seen by them (e.g.. newsletters, statements of philosophy, records and files). Such documents can reveal much about the recordkeepers and can add to the formulation of a total picture of a given phenomenon.

Interviewing in qualitative research refers to the process of conducting open-ended interviews in which both interviewer and respondent conduct a free interchange of thoughts and feelings. Areas that arise and that my not have been anticipated by the interviewer may be pursued in the interview. Categories of "meaning" may emerge in the course of the interview and become the data upon which an "understanding" is reached about the research question under study. The question is answered by the "self-report" type of data that is obtained by asking subjects what they think and feel about a given situation. The open-ended interview is the preferred method of obtaining such data in qualitative research because probing questions can be asked by a researcher who is also interacting with a subject and revealing his or her own feelings in the course of the interview. Such an interview technique may be used alone as the principal gathering technique or in combination with the participant observation technique. As in all qualitative research, the researcher is an integral part of the data gathering process and this is particularly true of the interview process which produces not only transcripts of the interview, but also the recorded impressions of the researcher about the subject and about the environment in which the interview took place. In summary, the qualitative interview technique will gather data that relies for its accuracy on a true representation of "what was said" and "how and in what context" it was said. (Ref. chapter on descriptive research re: open-ended questions.)

Analysis of Data

Data analysis is the process of pulling your facts together, tabulating them, sorting them, and deciding what they mean. Your major tasks are compiling, interpreting, and presenting information about your researchable problem. Before analysis, you have "raw data" that needs to be summarized and classified so that it makes sense to you and, to the audience for which it is intended. Your analysis may (in quantitative research) employ percentage tables, graphs, charts, or other methods of displaying the facts visually. When you analyze the facts, it is essential to refer back to either your tentative hypothesis or initial research question.

In a participant observation study, or document analysis procedure, or open-ended interview study, you or your team of investigators should meet frequently during the fact-finding process in order to draw inferences, raise new questions, and adjust the scope, focus or schedule of observations accordingly. The data will confirm or suggest questions for exploration and vantage points for gathering further data. It is an inductive process which moves from recording specific facts to compiling a series of facts, to interpreting the facts.

In analyzing qualitative data, the following questions are appropriate to consider:

1. Does the evidence support/reject particular answers to research questions?
2. What new questions does the evidence raise? Should we attempt to answer them? Should other leads be pursued or other clues tracked down?
3. How does the data, developed through qualitative techniques, tie into other relevant information? (A multi-method approach is appropriate to help answer difficult questions and present a persuasive report in which facts, figures, descriptive analysis, and other information are built into a compeling case and set of proposals.)

General Interview Techniques

I. **What Makes a Good Interviewer?** Have a positive:
   1. Attitude (you feel study is important, etc.)
   2. Establish rapport—interaction must be pleasant and satisfying. Be positive and self-assured,
   3. Dress appropriately—suitable to neighborhood or setting into which you will go.
   4. Have proper tools: sharp pencil, writing tablet, tape recorder pre-tested.

II. **Interviewing Techniques**
   1. Tell who you are and have information about the the study clearly in hand to stimulate interest.
   2. Mention confidentiality of information.
   3. Tell how respondent was chosen.
   4. Suggest course of action you want. Do not give option to refuse.
   5. Be prepared to answer questions.

III. Beginning the Interview

1. Avoid an audience/stress privacy.
2. Search for appropriate seating arrangements. Respondent should be sitting across from you.
3. Try to get your interview—be flexible.
4. Begin questioning promptly.

IV. Develop a Good Interviewing Relationship

1. Be genuinely interested and accepting.
2. Develop permissive atmosphere.
3. Develop freedom from pressure or coercion—no impatience.
4. Never let interview be threatening—"you must have an opinion on that".

V. Asking Questions

1. Read exactly as worded (unless it is an open-ended interview).
2. Pace according to respondent's ability to comprehend. Re-read anything not understood.
3. Do not change order of questions. Some are strategically placed.
4. Put respondent at ease—no rush.
5. Do not let respondent read questions beforehand.

Figure 1-1
Characteristics of Qualitative
and Quantitative Research

Qualitative

<u>Phrases Associated with the Approach</u>

- ethnographic
- field work
- soft data
- symbolic interaction
- inner perspective
- naturalistic
- ethnomethodological
- descriptive

- participant observation
- phenomenological
- Chicago school
- documentary
- life history
- case study
- ecological

<u>Key Concepts Associated with the Approach</u>

- meaning
- common sense understanding
- bracketing
- definition of situation
- everyday life

- understanding
- process
- negotiated order
- for all practical purposes
- social construction

Quantitative

<u>Phrases Associated with the Approach</u>

- experimental
- hard data
- outer perspective
- empirical

- positivist
- social facts
- statistical

<u>Key Concepts Associated with the Approach</u>

- variable
- operationalize
- reliability
- hypothesis

- validity
- statistically significant
- replication

Qualitative

Names Associated with the Approach

Max Weber	Herbert Blumer
Charles Horton Cooley	W. I. Thomas
Harold Garfinkel	Everett Highes
Margaret Mead	Erving Goffman
Anselm Strauss	Harry Wolcott
Eleanor Leacock	Rosalie Wax
Harold S. Becker	George Herbert Mead
Raymond Rist	Barney Glaser
Estelle Fuchs	Hugh Mehan

Data

- descriptive
- personal documents
- field notes
- photographs
- people's own words
- official documents and other artifacts

Sample

- small
- nonrepresentative
- theoretical sampling

Techniques or Methods

- observation
- reviewing various documents and artifacts
- participant observation
- open-ended interviewing

Quantitative

Design

- structured, predetermined, formal, specific
- design is a detailed plan of operation

Written Research Proposals

- extensive
- detailed and specific in focus
- detailed and specific in procedures
- thorough review of substantive literature

Quantitative (continued)
Data
- quantitative
- quantifiable coding
- counts, measures

- operationalized variables
- statistical

Sample
- large
- stratified
- control groups
- precise

- random selection
- control for extraneous
  variables

Techniques or Methods
- experiments
- survey research
- structured interviewing

- quasi experiments
- structured observation
- data sets

Qualitative
Relationship with Subjects
- empathy
- emphasis on trust
- equalitarian

- intense contact
- subject as friend

Theoretical Affiliation
- symbolic interaction
- ethnomethodology
- phenomenology

- culture
- idealism

Academic Affiliation
- sociology
- history

- anthropology

Goals
- develop sensitized concepts
- describe multiple realities

- grounded theory
- develop understanding

Quantitative
Names Associated with the Approach

Emile Durkheim	Fred Kerlinger
Lee Cronback	Edward Thorndike
L. Guttman	Fred McDonald
Gene Glass	David Krathwohl
Robert Travers	Donald Campbell
Robert Bales	Peter Rossi

Theoretical Affiliation

- structural functionalism
- realism, positivism
- behavioralism
- logical empiricism
- systems theory

Academic Affiliation

- psychology
- economics
- sociology
- political science

Goals

- theory testing
- establish the facts
- statistical description
- show relationships
- between variables
- prediction

Qualitative
Design

- evolving, flexible, general
- design is a hunch as to how you might proceed

Written Research Proposals

- brief
- speculative
- suggest areas research may be relevant to
- often written after some data has been collected
- not extensive in substantive literature review
- general statement of approach

Qualitative (continued)

Instruments and Tools
- tape recorder
- transcriber

(the researcher is often the only instrument)

Problem in Using the Approach
- time consuming
- data reduction difficult
- reliability

- procedures not standardized
- difficult studying large population

Quantitative

Relationship with Subjects
- circumscribed
- short-term
- stay detached

- distant
- subject researcher

Instruments and Tools
- inventories
- questionnaires
- indexes

- computers
- scales
- test scores

Data Analysis
- deductive
- occurs at conclusion of data collection

- statistical

Problems in Using the Approach
- controlling other variables
- reification

- obtrusiveness

The most frequently used methods for collecting qualitative data are participant observation, the use of documents, and open-ended interviewing.

Participant observation is the most frequently used method in qualitative research. It is a field work technique of gathering evidence (data).

The participant observer goes into the setting or environment of the subjects or situation which is under study. The participant observer is both a researcher (taking notes in a systematic fashion) and a participant in the situation which he is endeavoring to understand. The method requires a great deal of time spent in the setting and copious field notes or other written record of what happens as well as other forms of descriptive data. The participant observer attempts to learn from his subjects and their environment and yet not necessarily be like the subjects.

Qualitative methodology calls for imagination, sensitivity and creativity in order to get the most out of it. Now there are kinds of problems that are clearly inappropriate for qualitative methodology. But there is a very important place for qualitative research in the understanding of human behavior and social processes. The qualitative researcher may absorb a lot of information that, at the time, may seem irrelevant and yet if his perspective on the situation changes, the information my turn out to be extremely valuable. The survey researcher limits himself to what he considers important at the outset. The fieldworker can easily move back and forth from data gathering in the field to analysis at his desk. He has less of an investment to discard if he started out on the wrong track than the survey researcher does. In addition, difficult to quantify variables are probably less distorted by unstructured observation and interviewing than by an abortive effort to operationalize them for quantification by a survey.

A qualitative research study often defies standardized research procedure and as a consequence, many scientists remain unconvinced of the quality of the data and of the conclusions arrived at. Such questions deserve serious consideration and the answers are quite difficult to establish for the standard means of ascertaining the validity and reliability of data—collection operations are largely not applicable to such a study design. In order to obtain an accurate and reasonably complete analytic description of some social organization or situation, the qualitative researcher must employ his generally accepted techniques (most social scientists accept the utility of observation, interviewing, document analysis) in an adequate way. This means employing qualitative studies that often suggest hypotheses to be tested.

A second major limitation flows from the researcher's use of the relationship he establishes in the field, that is, the likelihood of bias. There is great danger that the researcher will guide the inquiry in accord with wrong impressions he has gotten from the first informant contacted or he may receive an endless amount of information from persons who are biased toward one point of view. In compensation, the researcher is not bound by prejudgment as the survey researcher; the qualitative researcher can reformulate the problem as he goes along. Because of his close contact with his respondent, he is also better able to avoid misleading or meaningless questions because he can reformulate them. He is also able to classify respondents more reliably than a rigid index drawing upon one or two questions in a questionnaire. A fieldworker can constantly modify his categories, making them more suitable for the analysis of the problem he is studying. The survey researcher is often stuck with the categories or variables he originally used in conceiving the problem. The qualitative researcher can generally refute motives more validly by contrasting stated ideals with actual behaviors supplemented by the informant's reactions to "feedback." Here, the researcher describes the informant's motives as they appear to him for corroboration or modification. The fieldworker can generally get indepth material more satisfactorily than the survey researcher. He can cultivate a relationship with the respondent and draw out depth material when the respondent is ready for it.

The characteristics of qualitative research may be summarized as follows:

Qualitative research is often carried out in natural or field settings. The environment in which a person lives or in which an activity takes place becomes a primary source for data collection and the researcher becomes the primary data-collecting instrument. Data is gathered on location by means of field notes or video tapes, or tape-recorded interviews, or the direct quotes of "what people said" by the recall ability of the researcher after he leaves the setting. The significance of a word or gesture in the research study is seen "in context" by the researcher who must often employ his or her own insight in understanding that which is under study in its own setting (e.g., an evaluation of a school would entail repeated visits to various sites, such as the cafeteria, as well as recorded impressions of both teachers and students as they interact in the school setting).

Qualitative research collects descriptive data in the form of words or pictures rather than numbers. The written presentation of the study will include direct quotations or personal documents (e.g., diary or biography), interview transcripts, videotapes, or other official records. In other words, an attempt, is made to "picture" the subject in context so that a comprehensive understanding can be arrived at about the phenomena under study. Significance in the research sense, equals understanding from the person's perspective or presenting an accurate picture of a setting divorced from its own, taken for granted, assumptions.

Qualitative research attempts to show the process that occurs when people define their meanings of the world in which they live, rather than such end products of the process such as outcomes or products. For example, quantitative techniques can show, by means of pre and post-testing, "that" changes occur in a setting. Qualitative strategies can suggest how change may have come about by studying such things as the assumptions or predispositions of subjects or settings that led to change. The subjective states of individuals would be seen as significantly related to the process of change in an individual or setting. The job of the qualitative researcher would be to present an accurate picture of these subjective factors.

Unlike quantitative research strategies, qualitative research does not search for evidence to prove or disprove an "already" held hypothesis, although that may sometimes be the case. Very often, a case built for an hypothesis or a theory is based on data that has been gathered inductively or building up to an hypothesis or theory about some given under study. The picture takes shape after gathering the data or begins to emerge as the data is being gathered. This allows a great deal of flexibility in such a research study as the data collection may be redirected at any point in the study. Quantitative studies are highly structured and often do not allow for this type of flexibility.

In summary, the qualitative researcher is interested in such questions as: What assumptions do people make about their lives? What do they take for granted? The concern of this type of research is to secure the perspectives of people accurately as they define their own sphere of meaning. Such data can be validated by actually showing that which has been collected to participants for feedback or by having someone other than the researcher check the reliability of the findings or even subject the results of the qualitative inquiry to verification by conducting a quantitative study. Qualitative and quantitative methods may be combined in same cases, or one type of study may use the methodology of the other in order to enhance the investigation of the question under scrutiny. However, it must be remembered that both methodologies proceed from different underlying assumptions.

Chapter 5

Qualitative Study—The West End: An Urban Village*

Herbert Gans

Overview

To the average Bostonian, the West End was one of the three slum areas that surrounded the city's central business district, little different in appearance and name from the North or the South End. He rarely entered the West End and usually glimpsed it only from the highways or elevated train lines that enveloped it. From there he saw a series of narrow winding streets flanked on both sides by columns of three- and five-story apartment buildings, constructed in an era when such buildings were called tenements. Furthermore, he saw many poorly maintained structures, some of them unoccupied or partially vacant, some facing on alleys covered with more than an average amount of garbage; many vacant stores and enough of the kinds of people who are thought to inhabit a slum area.

To the superficial observer, armed with coventional images and a little imagination about the mysteries thought to lie behind the tenement entrances, the West End certainly had all the earmarks of a slum. Whether or not it actually was a slum is question that involves a number of tech-

* Source: Abridged from Herbert Gans, Urban Villagers (New York: Free Press,1962), pp. 3-18, 36-40, 80-89. Reprinted with permission.

nical housing and planning considerations and some value judgments. For the moment, the West End can be described simply as an old, somewhat deteriorated, low-rent neighborhood that housed a variety of people, most of them poor.

In most American cities there are areas where European immigrants—and more recently Negro and Puerto Rican ones—try to adapt their nonurban institutions and cultures to the urban milieu. Thus they may be called urban villages. The West End was an urban village.

In this particular urban village, the population's socio-economic level was low. Indeed, the sample's median income was just under $70 per week. About a quarter earned less than $50 per week; a half between $50 and $99; and the top category, slightly less than a fifth, between $100 and $175. Most of the household heads were unskilled or semiskilled manual workers (24 and 37 per cent respectively).[3] Skilled manual workers, semiskilled white-collar workers, and skilled white-collar workers (including small businessmen) each accounted for about 10 per cent of the sample.

Life in the West End

Until the coming of redevelopment,[2] only outsiders were likely to think of the West End as a single neighborhood. After redevelopment was announced, the residents were drawn together by the common danger, but, even so, the West End never became a cohesive neighborhood.

My first visit to the West End left me with the impression that I was in Europe. Its high buildings set on narrow, irregularly curving streets, its Italian and Jewish restaurants and food stores, and the variety of people who crowded the streets when the weather was good—all gave the area a foreign and exotic flavor. At the same time, I also noticed the many vacant shops, the vacant and therefore dilapidated tenements, the cellars and alleys strewn with garbage and the desolation on a few streets that were all but deserted.

After a few weeks of living in the West End, my observations and my perception of the area—changed drastically. The search for an apartment quickly indicated that the individual units were usually in much better condition than the outside or the hallways of the buildings. Subsequently, in wandering through the West End, and in using it as a resident, I developed a kind of selective perception, in which my eye focused only on those parts of the area that were actually being used by the people. Vacant buildings and boarded-up stores were no longer so visible, and the totally deserted alleys or streets were outside of the set of paths normally traversed, either by myself or by the West Enders. The dirt and spilled-over garbage remained, but, since they were concentrated in street gutters and empty lots, they were not really harmful to anyone and thus were not as noticeable as during my initial observations.

The Italians of the West End

This study concerns second-generation Italians[3]—the American born children of parents who came from Italy—some from the Southern Italian provinces, others from Sicily. They now are adults, mainly in their late thirties and forties, who are raising their own children. The term "West Enders" will be used to refer to the second-generation Italian-Americans who lived in the West End.

The Structure of West End Society: An Introduction to the Peer Group Society

The life of the West Ender takes place within three interrelated sectors: the primary group, the secondary group, and the outgroup. The primary group refers to that combination of family and peer relationships which I shall call the peer group society. The secondary group refers to the small array of Italian institutions, voluntary organizations, and other social bodies which function to support the workings of the peer group society. This I shall call the community. I use this term because it, rather than the West End or Boston, is the West Ender's community. The outgroup, which I shall describe as the outside world, covers a variety of non-Italian institutions in the West End, in Boston, and in America that impinge on his life often unhappily, to the West Ender's way of thinking.

Although social and economic systems in the outside world are significant in shaping the life of the West Ender, the most important part of that life is lived within the primary group. National and local economic, social and political institutions may determine the West Ender's opportunities for income, work, and standard of living, but it is the primary group that refracts these outside events and thus shapes his personality and culture. Because the peer group society dominates his entire life, and structures his-relationship with the community and the outside world, I shall sometimes use the term to describe not only the primary relationships, but the West Enders' entire social structure as well.

The primary group is a peer group society because most of the West Enders' relationships are with peers, that is, among people of the same sex, age, and life-cycle status. While this society includes the friendships, cliques, informal clubs, and gangs usually associated with peer groups, it also takes in family life. In fact, during adulthood, the family is its most important component. Adult West Enders spend almost as much time with siblings, in-laws, and cousins—that is, with relatives of the same sex and age—as with their spouses, and more time than with parents, aunts, and uncles. The peer group society thus continues long past adolescence, and, indeed, dominates the life of the West Ender from birth to death. For this reason, I have coined the term "peer group society."

In order to best describe the dominance of the peer group principle in the life of the West Ender, it is necessary to examine it over a typical life cycle. The child is born into a nuclear family; at an early age, however, he or she—although girls are slower to do this than boys,—transfers increasing amounts of his time and allegiance to the peers he meets in the street and in school. This transfer may even begin long before the child enters school. Thus, one West Ender told me that when he wanted his two-year-old son to attend an activity at a local settlement house, bribery and threats were useless, but that the promise that he could go with two other young children on the block produced immediate assent.

From this time on, then, the West Ender spends the rest of his life in one or another peer group. Before or soon after they start going to school, boys and girls form cliques or gangs. In these cliques, which are sexually segregated, they play together and learn the lore of childhood. The sexually segregated clique maintains its hold on the individual until late adolescence or early adulthood.

Dating, the heterosexual relationship between two individuals that the middleclass child enters into after puberty—or even earlier—is much rarer among West Enders. Boys and girls may come together in peer groups to a settlement house dance or a clubroom. Even so, they dance with each other only infrequently. Indeed, at the teenage dances I observed, the girls danced mostly with each other and the boys stood in the corner—a peer group pattern that may continue even among young adults.

The hold of the peer group is broken briefly at marriage. During courtship, the man commutes between it and his girl. Female peer groups—always less cohesive than male—break up even more easily then, because the girl who wants to get married must compete with her peers for male friends and must be at their beck and call. At marriage, the couple leaves its peer groups, but after a short time, often following the arrival of the first child, they both re-enter peer group life.

Most often a new peer group is formed, consisting of family members and a few friends of each spouse. This group meets after working hours for long evenings of sociability. Although the members of the group are of both sexes, the normal tendency is for the men and women to split up, the men in one room and the women in another. In addition, husband and wife also may belong to other peer groups: work colleagues or childhood friends among the men, informal clubs of old friends that meet regularly among the women. In the West End, friendship ties seem to be formed mainly in childhood and adolescence, and many of them last throughout life.

But the mainstay of the adult peer group society is the family circle.[4] The circle is made up of collateral kin: in-laws, siblings, and cousins predominately. Not all family members are eligible for the peer group, but the rules of selection—which are informal and unstated—are based less on closeness of kinship ties than on compatibility. Family members come together if they are roughly of the same age, socio-economic level, and cultural background. How closely or distantly they are related is much less important than the possession of common interests and values. Even among brothers and sisters only those who are compatible are likely to see each other regularly. This combination of family members and friends seems to continue to function as a peer group for the rest of the life cycle.

The West End, in effect, may be viewed as a large network of these peer groups, which are connected by the fact that some people may belong to more than one group. In addition, a few individuals function as communicators between the groups, and thus keep them informed of events and attitudes important to them all.

The hold of the peer, group on the individual is very strong. Achievement and social mobility, for example are group phenomena. In the current generation, in which the Italian is still effectively limited to blue-collar work, atypical educational and occupational mobility by the individual is frowned upon. Children who do well in school are called "sissies, " and they cannot excel there and expect to remain in their peer group. Since allegiance to any one group is slight at this stage, however, the good student can drift into other peer groups until he finds one with compatible members. Should such peers be lacking, he may have to choose between isolation or a group that does not share his standards. Often, he chooses the latter.

Life in a peer group society has a variety of far-reaching social and psychological consequences. Pressure on man and wife affects the family structure, as does the willingness—or resignation—of the parents in relinquishing their children to their own peer group at an early age. The fact that individuals are accustomed to being with—and are more at ease with—members of their own sex means that their activities are cued primarily to reference groups of that sex. This may help to explain the narcissistic vanity among West End men, that is, their concern with clothes, and displays of muscular strength or virility. It also may help to explain the chaperoning of unmarried women, in fear that they will otherwise indulge in sexual intercourse. Not only does the separation of the sexes substitute for the development of internal controls that discourage the man from taking advantage of the woman, but they replace, as well, those controls that allow the woman to protect herself.

The peer group principle has even more important consequences for personality organization. Indeed, the role of the group in the life of the individual is such that he exists primarily in the group. School officials, for example, pointed out that teenagers were rough and active when they were with their peers, but quiet and remarkably mild and passive when alone. Their mildness is due to the fact that they exist only partially when they are outside the group. In effect, the individual personality functions best and most completely among his or her peers -a fact that has some implications for independence and dependence, conformity and individualism among the West Enders.

The Individual and the Group

West Enders live within the group; they do not like to be alone. Indeed, for most of them, people trained from childhood to function solely within the group, being alone brings discomfort and ultimately fear. The discomfort was expressed by housewives who got their housework done quickly so as to be able "to visit." It was expressed more strongly by people who feared that the destruction of the West End would tear them away from their group and leave them isolated. It was expressed perhaps most vividly by a corner boy who explained to his friends that a prison sentence was bad "because it separates you from friends and family."

Yet the peer group is important not only because it provides this much desired companionship and the feeling of belongingness, but because it also allows its members to be individuals, and to express that individuality. In fact, it is only within the peer group that people can do so. In the middle class, people can exist as individuals outside a group, and enter a group to accomplish personal as well as shared ends. Among the West Enders, however, people grow up within a group and use it to be individuals, with the result that this group cannot work together. This is the basic paradox of the peer group society.

Although the peer group is the most important entity in the West Ender's life, he is not merely a robot whose actions are determined by the group or the cultural tradition. In fact, peer group life in many ways is just the opposite of the cohesive and tightly-knit group that has served as a model for descriptions of primary relations in other societies. It is a spirited competition of individuals "Jockeying" for respect, power, and status. Indeed, to the outside observer, West Enders appear to be involved in a never ending dialectic; individual actions affect the group momentarily and are followed by restraints that bring them back, only to be succeeded by more individuating talk of behavior.

This is most visible among the teenage and young adult action-seekers. Within the group their behavior is a series of competitive encounters intended to assert superiority and skillfullness of one individual over the other, which take the form of card games, short physical scuffles, and endless verbal duels. Through bragging, teasing, wisecracking, and insulting, individuals express their own verbal strength and skill, while denigrating the characteristics and achievements of others. Only when there is a common opponent does the group coalesce, but even then this is not always likely to happen. For example, among the young adults whom I observed at a tavern where they hung out nightly, a basketball team broke up because the better players did not want to play on a team with the poorer ones, who would deny them the opportunity to display their individual talents.

While there is no physical competition among the adult groups, and even card games are rare, similar competition does exist, although in considerably muted form. Most of the competitive play takes place in conversation, through an exchange of anecdotes that display the story teller's exploits, and of jokes and wisecracks that entertain the group while making one person stand out. The exchange is not vicious, nor is it used by self-centered people to call attention to themselves, or to make others look bad. In fact, any attempt by an insecure person to build himself up in the group at others' expense is considered out of place. It is politely ignored in his presence, and harshly criticized when he is out of earshot.

Group members—be they adult or adolescent—display themselves to the group, to show their peers that they are as good if not slightly better than the rest, but then they yield the floor to the next person and allow him to do likewise. The purpose of this is to create mild envy among the rest of the group.

Two other expressions of West End individualism are the rejection of formal dependence on the group, and the emphasis on the mutual nature of obligations. despite the fact that West Enders live so much within a group, they feel that they cannot and do not want to depend on it for help. People say that "in the last analysis, you have to depend on yourself." They are loath to ask for favors from others, even within the family circle, and much more so from organized charity. The emphasis on independence is based partly on a realistic appraisal that others can extend only a limited amount of help, and that it would be unrealistic to depend on them. When economic deprivations strike one member of a low-income population, they are likely to hit others as well. Moreover, if other troubles arise, such as illness, they are apt to be serious ones. Although West Enders will offer and accept help, they do not—cherish being dependent on others. They want to remain independent, for accepting aid is thought to reflect on the strength of the individual, and is thus a reflection on self-respect which places the dependent person in an inferior position.

Moreover, giving and receiving—or help or gifts—involves the individual in a spiral of reciprocatory obligations. The obligation may be latent, in which case people feel a desire to give and receive, and enjoy the resulting reciprocity. Or it may be manifest, thus becoming a duty. In this case reciprocity can turn into a burden, and people try to escape involvement. This happens most often with representatives from the outside world, like welfare agencies and settlement houses, who want to give aid in exchange for deference or loyalty to institutions.

Among close friends and relatives, goods and services are exchanged freely and obligations remain latent, unless one or the other person falls seriously behind in reciprocating or unless the exchange becomes competitive. Should someone reciprocate with a more expensive gift than he originally received, he may be suspected of showing off, or of trying to make the other person look bad. If it continues, this can lead to an eventual alienation from the group.

When relationships are not close, obligations are manifest. For example, after a man had done some electrical work for his sister, she invited him to dinner several times as payment—for the work—which he had done for nothing. Although she was not formally required to reciprocate, since he was her brother, she wanted to do so because she felt it to be the proper thing. This brother had married an upwardly mobile woman, and was not part of the immediate family circle.

When obligations concern authority figures and hierarchical relationships, the rejection of dependence becomes stronger, and often evolves into fear of domination. Thus, whereas West Enders will subordinate themselves to someone whom they recognize as a leader, they will bitterly reject the individual who is imposed as a leader from the outside— or who tries to impose himself.

Although the peer group is a theater for individual expression, it is also characterized by strict control of deviant behavior. The major mechanisms of social control are criticism, the expectation of criticism, and the not always successful attempts by individuals to maintain self-control.

Since everyone knows everyone else, life is an open book, and deviant acts are hard to hide. This means that such acts are committed either outside the reaches of the group as in the case of adolescents who do their misbehaving outside the West End—or that they are not committed at all. Jokes and wisecracks, a polite way of questioning deviant behavior, usually suffice to bring the individual back into line. Similarly, the individual is expected to keep up with the activities of the group, and the pattern of individual display. The person who is too noisy or dominating is suspect, but so is the one who is too quiet. The hostess who sets too lavish a table is criticized, but even more so is the person who is unwilling to entertain or feed the group in the style to which it is accustomed.

But as so much of life is based on routine, there is little incentive for non-conforming behavior. Thus most conformity is quite voluntary. But West Enders also regulate their conduct by involuntary conformity of the type expressed in the phrase "what will the neighbors think." Indeed, the expectations of what other people will think are extremely harsh; they assume the blackest thoughts and deeds possible. For example, a neighbor who had recently had a baby carried the baby carriage up several flights, rather than leaving it in an empty store that served as storage room for several adjacent apartment buildings. She justified her behavior by explaining that, since the storage room was not in her own building, people might think she was going in there to steal something. When the exaggerated expectations do constitute a potent control against deviant behavior, they create, at the same time, an unspoken atmosphere of mutual recrimination, in which everyone is likely to expect the worst from everyone else. It must be noted, however, that such expectations are usually not held about peer group members, but only about people who are less close—neighbors, for example.

It is clear that the ascription of evil motives and deeds stems not from observations of the neighbors' behavior or inferences from their conversations, but from the individual himself. He projects in the neighbors his underlying fear that he himself might do evil things or harbor evil motives. For although West Enders believe that fate regulates actions over which they have no say, their own behavior is thought to be self-determined.

The West Ender therefore is frequently concerned over his ability to control himself. Among the adolescents and the action-seeking adults, the main concern is to stay out of "trouble"—which means not only to avoid getting caught by the police or by other agents of social control, but also not going out of control in episodic behavior, for this might detach the individual from the group. Among routine-seeking people, uncontrolled behavior is less of a problem. Their concern is to avoid getting into situations that could be misinterpreted. In short, the individual must control himself so that he cannot be suspected of negatively evaluated behavior, either by the group or by himself.

The definition of deviant behavior comes initially from the group itself and the group encourages individuals to shame each other into conformity through overt criticism. In view of the severity of social control, it would be easy to caricature peer group life as a prison for its members. To the outsider, the concern with social control and self-control might indeed seem oppressive. But he must also take into account that there is little desire for voluntary nonconformity, and, consequently, little need to require involuntary conformity. Nor do people seem to be troubled by fears about the breakdown of self-control, or about the possibility that they may be suspected of misdeeds. Although these potentialities do lurk under the surface, they do not usually disturb the positive tenor of group relations. Such fears, of course, may be private preoccupations, less visible to the sociologist than they would be to the clinical psychologist. Moreover, the people who are not seriously troubled by these fears shun the kind of group I have discussed.

Tensions and problems exist in the peer group, as in every other group, but they are overshadowed by the gratifications that it provides for the individual. Perhaps the best illustration of this was given by a young man who was suffering from an ulcer, and was faced with a choice between his health and his group. As he explained it: "I can't stop drinking when I'm with my friends; I eat and drink like they do and when I'm alone I take care of my ulcer. But I don't care if it kills me; if it does, that's it."

In summary, social relationships within the peer group follow a narrow path between individualistic display and strictly enforced social control. The group is set up to provide its members with an opportunity for displaying, expressing, and acting out their individuality, as long as this does not become too extreme.

As a result, the peer group is unable to work together to achieve a common goal unless it is shared by all members of the group. Since the main function of the group is to provide an area for individual display, the members are less interested in activities that require working together than in impressing each other. Moreover, if group tasks, especially those of a good nature, are suggested, people become fearful that they will be used as pawns by an individual who will gain the most from this activity. Consequently, the inability to participate in joint activities does inhibit community organization, even when it concerns the very survival of the group, as it did in the clearance of the West End. This, perhaps, is the peer group society's most serious weakness: that the group is used by its members to express and display individualistic strivings and that these strivings prevent the group from acting in concert.

Suggested Questions for Evaluating a Qualitative Study—in this case—Participant Observation

Area I

- Are processes by which data gathered described?
- Have hypotheses been formulated?
- Have observers influenced the beliefs and actions of those observed?
- Is there any check on the reliability of the observers' classification of incidents in regard to an emerging theory?
- Does the researcher overidentify with his informants?
- Were his interactions with informants controlled?
- Have observers influenced the beliefs and actions of those observed?

Area II—Procedures

- Have biases of the researcher been stated?
- Are there limitations on the data collected? Have they been stated?
- Are relevant indicators in the material gathered seen as related to the main theory or pattern being proposed by the study?
- Is the problem defined? Were any provisional hypotheses formulated?
- Does the observer describe his role in relation to the group?
- Was anything said on possible "effects of being observed"?

Area III—Results

- Does the study seem to fulfill the assumptions of qualitative research?
- How were findings analyzed?
- What patterns emerged from the observer's research? Were they clearly stated?
- Is the study open to further research? Does it call for further research?

Area IV—Ethical Considerations

- ex. the role of participant observer (or "covert observer in disguise") has been criticized for its ethical implications.
- Would it benefit subjects studied?
- What facts does the researcher have a right to make public?
- Who sponsored the research? What was its purpose?

Area V—Speculative Area

- What guidelines can be established to evaluate qualitative studies?

Notes

1. These figures report the occupation of the past or present household head. In 18 per cent of the cases, the woman's occupation is reported, either because there was never a male household head, the husband was not in the labor force because of illness, or because his occupation was unavailable.

2. The West End had been slated for slum clearance since the early 1950s and was torn down shortly after my fieldwork ended in 1958. It was rebuilt with luxury high-rise housing, and all of the West Enders had to move elsewhere; none could afford the rents in the new development. The West Enders' reaction to the destruction of their neighborhood is described in detail in Chapters 13 and 14 of Urban Villagers.

3. The Center for Community Studies survey indicates that they made up 42 per cent of the West End population. They comprised 55 per cent of all second generation residents.

4. I have borrowed this term from Michael Young and Peter Willmott, Family and Kinship in East London, London: Routledge and Kegan Paul, 1957.

Chapter 6

Evaluation Research

E valuation is the application of research skills to determine the worth of an educational practice. Evaluation may have an immediate effect on decision-making in a given setting or attempt to provide knowledge for decisions regarding the adoption of materials on procedures by a given organization.

Evaluation skills include abilities to analyze the practice to be evaluated, acquire a knowledge of the environmental context and the values operating in the site, work with diverse evaluation audiences, and communicate technical data in a non-threatening and understandable fashion. A practitioner of evaluation research is both a researcher and a concerned educator whose efforts are essential to the effective functioning of organizations. Evaluation, as defined from a research orientation, requires both a formal evaluation design and procedures that will systematically collect and analyze in order to determine the value of a specific educational practice that currently exists or one intended for future implementation.

Types of Evaluation

There are two types of evaluation efforts that affect the evaluation process in a given setting. FORMATIVE EVALUATION collects data in order to modify or revise a curriculum in a developmental stage. The research questions appropriate to formative evaluation are, "How can this be taught better?" "Does the curriculum achieve its objectives?" The results of this type of evaluation effort may lead to a decision to revise a curriculum, gather more data through field testing or further development of a program or policy.

SUMMATIVE EVALUATION determines the effectiveness of a program, especially in comparison with other programs. Summative evaluation can be conducted once a program is fully operating. The research questions asked in summative evaluation involve such considerations as, "which of several programs achieves certain objectives most effectively and efficiently?" Such evaluation efforts can help educators who make purchase or adoption decisions regarding new programs, products, or procedures.

The distinction that has been made between formative and summative evaluation is important because it has ramifications for the entire evaluation effort that one may wish to employ. Formative evaluation is frequently done by an on-site or internal evaluator who is often a member of a team. Formative evaluation data frequently employs such methods as observation, interviews, questionnaires and other on-site developed methods. Such research considerations as control, statistical equivalence of groups and generalizability of findings are not of primary importance.

Summative evaluation is usually done by an external evaluator who has no vested interest in the setting being evaluated. Summative evaluation data is usually collected using standardized instruments with high validity and reliability. Summative evaluation places high priority on research control, statistical equivalence of groups, and generalizability of findings.

These two types of evaluation may frequently overlap in an individual study as evaluation designs are influenced by the needs of those being evaluated, their individual practices, and the feasibility of implementing the findings of the evaluation. Unlike basic research which seeks to develop theory and scientific knowledge, evaluation research seeks an immediate practical use of its findings in the situation which it was called upon to evaluate. This consideration will influence our further discussion of evaluation in the material below.

Stages in Conducting Evaluation Research

Evaluation research tries to establish how successful a program of action is in achieving its goal of dealing with a particular program. In the stage of formulating the problem and articulating a program to deal with that problem, the evaluation researcher should ideally be involved from the outset. However, this is rarely the case. In evaluation, the problem situation should (1) be as specific as possible and (2) potential causes of the problem should be spelled out as clearly as possible.

The next stage in the evaluation effort will be the formulation of a research design that can determine the effectiveness of a program. The ideal model is the controlled experiment but other approaches are more frequently used because of the difficulty of implementing a controlled experiment in on-site investigations. Educational settings are not often a condusive atmosphere for the expected rigor of the experimental design. Controlled experiments are not always necessary for good evaluation research.

The third stage in the evaluation research process is the implementation of the research design. This stage in the process can often encounter opposition from on-site personnel who may feel that their program is being adversely affected by the evaluation or who may feel threatened in general by the presence of outside evaluators. One way of alleviating this situation is to involve program personnel in the research and evaluation process itself.

The final stage of the evaluation research process is the utilization of the results for decision-making. The results have to be framed in a non-threatening way and presented in a positive and constructive way. Decision-makers should be identified and presented with the facts so that improvement can take place.

How You Go About Conducting Evaluation Research*

I. As an evaluator you have to know for *whom* you are writing.
    A. Identify relevant decision-makers—those to whom your report will be directed. The data and information you produce is to provide a means of making enlightened decision-making in a program.

---

* Reprinted from Issac, Stephen and Michael, William B., *Handbook In Research And Evaluation, California; Edits, 1977.*

    B. Know the policy decision-making processes, e.g., know agency personnel, community groups, to whom the program is addressed.

II. GOALS

1) identify and clarify the decision-makers *goals* for these are often the same as the goals of the program to be evaluated.
2) most programs have multiple goals and these should be dealt with in a *priority* from *most* important to least important. These goals become part of the evaluation strategy. Maybe only *major goals* will be evaluated.
3) help decision-makers *operationalize* their goals—in other words—help decision-makers clarify in concrete terms what they want to accomplish.

    a) identify the possible goals
    b) consider the consequences of undertaking alternate courses of action.
    c) highlight conflicting goals

EVALUATION RESEARCH INVOLVES MEASURING RELATIVE DEGREES OF GOAL ATTAINMENT

III. In Evaluation, the next step after goal identification is identification of
1) relevant input variables.
2) articulation of decision-makers' theory.

This stage in the process answers the question: WHY and HOW are the goals expected to be attained? For example, in regard to identifying input variables—There is a theory that if people participate in a common experience—discussion will be enhanced and that people learn more by actually doing something than by simply learning about it. This means that our *input variables* would focus on the *degree to which people actually took part in an exercise* designed to put the mentioned theory into practice. We might also look at the degree to which they took it seriously, and the degree to which they actually followed instructions—as part of your evaluation you should help articulate the theory behind a program so that it can be tested in the real world in which the program operates.

Often people who design and implement social programs carry around with them vague and unarticulated theories about social causes.

IV. Decide how factors and variables in a program are to be *measured*. Ways in which input factors and goals are measured must make sense to your decision-makers. These measures although reliable and valid must be *understandable* if decision-makers are to be committed to the results of your research. What the decision-maker wants to know should be taken into account in what you measure about a program.

V. Formulate a Research Design and Methodology: sample size, groups to be sampled, case study, experimental design, observation, interviews, questionnaires, tests, etc.

- Traditional Research Strategies can be found in, *Experimental + Quasi-Experimental Designs for Research* by Campbell and Stanley.
- Qualitative Methods can be found in *Analyzing Social Settings* by John Lofland.

Take into account that the results must make sense to project directors and must meet their needs and values.

VI. *Analysis of Data*—should be kept separate from *Interpretation* of the data. In other words—*here* is my data—no evaluative judgments are contaminating the data presentation. Data is such that anyone can take it and make their own judgments.

VII. We have talked about an interactive evaluative process with both decision-makers and you as instructors involved in a common effort. Feedback should be stressed and stressed as a 1) continual process and 2) sometimes informal (e.g., meetings) and 3) sometimes formal feedback (e.g., written reports, conferences, workshops).

This feedback should be reported in a way that makes sense to the audience to which it is aimed. For lay audiences—sophisticated statistical reports may be meaningless.

As evaluators, you have your optimal impact when you can be understood and your reports are used by program people to improve what they are doing. This attitude guides your research best—from beginning to end.

Chapter 7

Evaluation Studies—Dropout Factors in the Process of Influencing Classroom Change Through Teacher Education

Ladd Holt and Don Uhlenberg

Evaluation Study

New and innovative approaches to teaching in elementary schools are often advocated by university teacher education programs but fail to reach the classroom. Using a conceptual model of six drop-out factors, the study investigated the effects of an innovative approach to mathematics teaching at the University of Utah on the teaching practices of its graduates. Data revealed that teachers were using the approach to teaching mathematics learned as undergraduates to a moderate degree and that the primary reason given for not employing such a method more was that they never learned how to organize and manage the total classroom so that the new approach, which required small group and individual instruction could be utilized. School system resistance was not found to be as important a factor in use of innovative methods as is popularly believed.

A continuing and critical concern of teacher education professors is the effect of pre-service teacher education on the practices of graduates, especially when the teacher training program advocates methods of teaching that are not commonly used in the public schools. The hope, if not the conviction, of most education professors is that the attitudes, values, methods, and techniques taught in their university classes will, when implemented in the public schools, result in more valuable learning experiences for children. The results, however, have not always been encouraging. The classroom practices of most beginning teachers are more apt to resemble those of the teacher next door than those of university instructors.

Investigation of this phenomena has not been easy for researchers. The complexity of the teacher education process itself makes accurate assessment a formidable task as the factors involved are difficult to isolate and identify for purposes of examining cause and effect relationships. Consequently, the reasons generally given as to why teacher education professors are or are not successful influencing the behavior of classroom teachers reflect, perhaps, more subjective speculation than objective investigation.

The mathematics education portion of the University of Utah elementary education program had, for some time, advocated a unique approach to the teaching of math and contained all the essential ingredients for bringing about change in the teaching of mathematics. This paper presents a model for assessing why knowledge and skills presented to future teachers as part of their professional training are not used and, within the area of elementary school math, provides the results of an initial test of the model.

Background and Purpose

Elementary education students take two courses designed to prepare them to teach math. The first course (Math 405) uses concrete models that can be manipulated by students to gain understanding of the mathematical rules which are a part of the elementary school curriculum. A discovery approach, where the professors give problems and ask questions which can be solved by the manipulation of concrete models and where students work in small groups sharing answers, is utilized.

The focus is not on finding "right answers" but rather on the ability to demonstrate how the rules operate in the concrete world. The second course (ED 518) helps students use the methods learned within the content course. Also students work with individual or small groups of children where the emphasis is placed on assisting future teachers with understanding how children think mathematically together with the questioning skills to pose problems and questions which will extend the math thinking. A clearly articulated approach to the teaching and learning of mathematics has been developed and is applied in this program (Jencks & Peck, 1975; 1968).

Students have opportunities to experience the Jencks-Peck approach both as learners and as teachers; and most students seem to understand and accept it as a superior way of performing mathematics. Yet, general impressions of the elementary faculty as well as the mathematics instructors themselves indicated that the approach taught at the university (hereafter referred to as the Jencks-Peck approach) was not being implemented to any great extent by student teachers or graduates in their teaching.

The purposes of this research were as follows: a) to study the extent to which graduates of the elementary teacher education program were using the Jencks-Peck approach in the teaching of mathematics in their classrooms b) to investigate the reasons why those who were not using the approach or only using the approach partially were not incorporating it in their teaching to a greater extent; and c) to determine whether any differences existed in the responses to the factors by teachers who had been teaching for different lengths of time.

A basic assumption of the study was that there would be a sufficient number of teachers who were using the Jencks-Peck approach only partially or not at all to warrant investigation as to the reasons why the approach was not adopted more fully. It was reasoned that somewhere between the initial exposure to the Jencks-Peck approach in Math 405 and the time when the teacher began teaching, there existed a number of obstacles or barriers, any one of which might serve as a block to the implementation of the approach. These were labeled "dropout factors."

Initially it was thought that these factors might be sequential and that passing or completing each would be a requisite for going on to the next. Had this been so, these factors would have been considered as "dropout stages," thus providing a temporal model for assessing points at which students could be judged as eligible or ineligible as potential implementers of the Jencks-Peck approach. Subsequent discussion suggested that this would probably not be the case and that a student might skip one factor only to pick it up at a later stage, out of sequence. Nevertheless, it seemed probable that all six factors must be met if the student were to use the Jencks-Peck approach to any great extent. To state it another way, the basic assumption was that: there were six conditions that must be successfully met before teachers would use the knowledge and skills learned in teacher education programs in the classroom.

Dropout Factors

1. Knowledge and understanding of the basic concepts and principles of mathematics as taught by Jencks and Peck. A student may, because of laziness, lack of motivation, low intellectual capability, etc. never grasp the essence of mathematics from this point of view.

   Such a lack of understanding would preclude both subsequent success in the program as well as future implementation in the classroom.

2. Perception of the Jencks-Peck approach as a personally valuable way to learn mathematics. A student, while understanding the approach and performing adequately in the processes, might not regard this method as any better (and perhaps even less valuable) than the traditional ones of memorizing formulae and computing answers to mathematical problems.

3. Belief that the Jencks-Peck approach is one that could and/or should be-used in teaching mathematics in the elementary school. Because of personal beliefs regarding the goals of mathematics education or ideas about the motivation or intellectual ability of elementary school aged children, a student might see the Jencks-Peck approach as not suitable for elementary schools even though he may value it personally.

4. Attainment of a level of competency in teaching mathematics to children individually or in small groups using the Jencks-Peck approach. Teaching this approach required a somewhat unique set of attitudes and teaching techniques on the part of the student. For a number of reasons, the student may not possess the basic personality, attitudes or abilities to be successful in learning to teach the Jencks-Peck approach.

5. Acquisition of the necessary skills for organizing and managing the classroom so that the Jencks-Peck approach could be taught. Because this approach required the teacher to teach

children in a one to one or small group situation, the future teacher must learn to manage a classroom of 25 to 35 children in order to be free to teach the Jencks-Peck approach without losing control aver the activities of the rest of the class.

6. Resistance by the school system to the implementation of the Jencks-Peck approach when the student secures a teaching position. Curriculum mandates, pressures from the principal, supervisor, and other school people, resistance from children and parents all were potential sources which may prevent the teacher from implementing such a mathematics program.

Procedures and Results

Forty-eight teachers who met the following criteria of the study were located:

1) had taken both Math 405 and Education 518 with either Jencks and/or Peck in the previous 5 years.
2) were currently teaching in an elementary school in one of three districts in the Salt Lake Valley, Utah.

Of the 48 questionnaires sent, 28 (56%) were completed and returned. The characteristics of those returning and not returning the questionnaire were similar. The moderate rate of return can be explained, in part, by the fact that the questionnaires were mailed late in the school year.

The first 6 questions on the questionnaire corresponded to the six dropout factors and the seventh dealt with the extent to which the Jencks-Peck approach was being implemented (see Table 7.1).

Table 7.1
Questions Included on the Teacher Questionnaire

---

1. How well do you think you learned and understood the math concepts taught in Math 405 and Education 518?

Not very well   1   2   3   4   5   Very well

2. To what extent do you think the approach to learning math as taught in Math 405 and Education 518 was of more value to you as a learner than other ways you've experienced?

Little value   1   2   3   4   5   Great value

3. To what extent do you think the approach to learning math as it was taught in Math 405 and Education 518 is applicable to the elementary school?

Little   1   2   3   4   5   Fully
applicability   applicable

4. Assuming you could work with children in small groups like those you worked with in Education 518 how well do you think that course prepared you to teach math to children?

Not very-well   1   2   3   4   5   Very well

5. As-a result of your university training, how prepared were you to organize your total classroom to incorporate a math program as taught in Education 518 into the total curriculum?

Minimally   1   2   3   4   5   Very well
prepared   Prepared

6. To what extent does the public school system in which you work prevent you from putting into operation a math program as taught in your university teacher education program?

Little   1   2   3   4   5   Highly
interference   restricted

7. To what extent do you believe you are-using a math approach as taught by Jencks and Peck in the Math 405 and Education 518 courses you took at the University of Utah?

very little		1	2	3	4	5		Fully

Respondents were asked to reply on a five-point scale with 1 indicating a generally low response and 5 a high. Space was provided for additional comments. Information regarding grade level and years of experience was also solicited.

Table 7.2 shows the median response for the 27 teachers on each of the seven factors of the questionnaire.

Table 7.2
Median Scores for Dropout and Implementation Factors

Factors	N	Median Score
1. Understanding of Concepts	27	4.00
2. Perceived Value	27	4.00
3. Belief in Applicability	27	3.00
4. Teaching Competency	27	4.00
5. Classroom Management Skill	27	2.00
6. School Resistance	27	3.00
7. Degree of implementation	27	3.00

The median response of 4.00 on a five point scale to factors 1, 2, and 4 indicated that teachers felt that they understood the fundamentals of mathematics (factor 1), that they valued the approach by which they were taught (factor 2), and that they had learned how to teach mathematics to small groups using the Jencks-Peck approach (factor 4).

The median score of 3.00 on factor number 3 showed a difference of opinion on how well teachers felt the approach was applicable for use in a public school classroom. The response to this factor by teachers was very similar to their response to factor 7 which indicated the extent to which they used the method in their own teaching practice. It was felt the extent to which they saw the Jencks-Peck approach as applicable was determined at least in part by the degree to which they were using the approach in their own teaching.

Teachers seemed to agree that what they had not learned in their pre-service teacher education program was how to organize a classroom of 30 or more students so that the small group approach required by the Jencks-Peck method could be used. The median score of 2 for factor 5 was the lowest of the median scores on the seven factors. The response to factor 5 was found to be significantly different statistically from the response to factor 1 using the Wilcoxon matched pairs signed-ranks test (T = 4.5, P .001).

Responses to factor 6 (median score of 3) showed that obstruction to the use of this innovative approach by the school system was varied. In the comments to this item, some teachers said that they were told what methods to use in teaching mathematics. Yet the comments seemed to indicate that the reasons preventing the use of the method were due more to large classes and to lack of time and materials. The responses to factor 6, therefore, seemed more related to lack of skill in organizing a classroom to use the Jencks-Peck approach than to specific directives by the school system on how mathematics was to be taught.

Factor 7, with a median score of 3, indicated that the approach was used moderately by teachers in their present teaching. Eight of the 27 teachers reported not using the approach at all and only one teacher reported using the approach fully. The pre-service teacher education program appeared to have some effect upon the way graduates teach mathematics but not as much as might be expected.

Years in Teaching and Item Response. Because of the mixed responses on items 3, 6, and 7, it was decided to investigate whether the response to these items was related to teaching experience. The 27 respondents were divided into three groups (1) those teaching for one year; (2) those teaching for two years; and (3) those who had taught between three and five years. Table 7.3 shows the median scores to items 3, 6, and 7 for each of the three groups.

Table 7.3
Median Scores of Teachers on Factors 3, 6, and 7
as Related to Years of Teaching Experience

Factors	Median score 1st year Teachers N=10	Median score 2nd year Teachers N=8	Median score 3rd to 5th year Teachers N=9
3. Belief in Applicability	2	3	4
6. School Resistance	4	2.5	2
7. Degree of Implementation	1.5	3	3

The responses to factor 3 indicated that the longer a person taught, the more applicability the Jencks-Peck approach seemed to have for use in the elementary school. First-year teachers (median =2.0) believed the approach had some applicability while persons teaching from three to five years thought it most applicable (median = 4.0). Using the Mann-Whitney U Test, the differences in medians of the first-year and second-year teachers were shown to be statistically significant (U=17.p .05). The median difference between the group of first-year teachers and the group that had been teaching for three to five years was also significant (U=22.p .05). statistically.

Examination of the response of the three groups to factor 6 showed that the group with more teaching experience saw less restriction placed upon their teaching of mathematics (median=2.0) than either second year (median=2.5) or first-year (median=4.0) teachers. Again the Mann-Whitney U Test was used to determine if the median differences were statistically significant. The differences between the first-year and the second-year teachers were significant (U=10.p .05). The differences between first-year teachers and teachers who had been teaching from three to five years were also statistically significant (U=18.p .05).

A study of responses to item 7 indicated that experienced teachers were more likely to use the Jencks-Peck approach than were teachers in their first year of teaching. The difference in median between the first-year and the second-year was statistically significant (U=14.p .05) and there was a statistically significant difference between the medians of the first-year teachers and those teaching from three to five years, (U=15.p .05).

Given the very small sample, the results reported above are only suggestive. The trends, however, are interesting in terms of the effect of teaching experience upon the use of teaching methods learned during pre-service education programs.

Correlation Between Drop-out Factors and Use. A major question considered was whether the response of teachers to the six dropout factors (items 1 through 6 on the questionnaire) was related to teacher use of the Jencks-Peck approach in teaching mathematics (item 7). A Spearman rank order correlation was computed to determine the relationship (rho-.77). The correlation was significant (t=6.09. p .0005). The moderately high correlation indicated that the six dropout factors in the questionnaire did account for a considerable proportion of the variance in the extent to which the Jencks-Peck approach was used by classroom teachers. From this, it can be assumed that the dropout factors used in the questionnaire were critical factors in determining whether or not the mathematics methods learned during pre-service teacher education were used during the teaching career of the graduate.

Written Comments. Written comments of the teachers generally supported the numerical rating made on each factor. Several comments described why the mathematics courses at the university were regarded as successful. The following is representative: It helped me learn to use my reasoning ability, to understand the theory behind a problem and not just the process of solution. Several teachers commented on the fact that they were intially afraid of mathematics and their experiences in the teacher education program had shown them that they could understand the subject matter and help children to learn.

Most of the negative comments concerned the problems associated with using the Jencks-Peck approach in regular classrooms. A typical response was: I've tried it. However, it's impractical for a 35 student classroom. Others criticized the teacher education program because nowhere in the program had they learned how to organize their classroom so that individual or small group instruction could be carried out. One teacher expressed this when she wrote, "I didn't find any class in the education program that taught me how to organize any part of a total classroom."

Conclusions and Implications

This study gives some support to the concept of the six dropout factors as a viable framework for investigating the reasons why skills, values and knowledge taught in a pre-service teacher education program might not reach classroom implementation. The study also suggests the addition of another factor, the number of years of teaching, as an important influence to be considered. By altering the wording of the questionnaire, data could be gathered on the effects of teacher education on classroom practice in other areas of the curriculum as well. Potentially, the concept of the six dropout factors could provide a powerful tool for identifying and isolating program gaps and weaknesses.

Although the sample was small, the survey did indeed identify an area of weakness in the mathematics education portion of theUniversity of Utah teacher education program. Classroom teachers revealed that though they understood, accepted, and valued the Jencks-Peck approach and even knew how to teach it to small groups of children, never were the teachers shown how to organize and manage their classrooms so the approach could be easily used in their math programs. The data suggest that the university has not paid sufficient attention to the realities of the public school classroom and especially the difficulty in organizing large numbers of children so that direct teaching can occur individually and in small groups. While there is an increased emphasis-upon field experience in the teacher education curriculum, the methods courses perhaps still focus too much upon ideal classroom situations. Also, not enough help is given to prospective teachers on how to organize so that small group teaching methods can be used within classrooms containing large numbers of children.

The effect of teaching experience on responses to the questionnaire, especially items 3, 6, and 7, was not expected and raises a number of interesting questions about when teachers might use the knowledge and skills they learned in professional preparation. First-year teachers may be too concerned with the issue of survival-in the classroom to use any approach that might be considered innovative either by other faculty in the school or by the children being taught. Only as teachers become more secure in their ability to manage classrooms and meet the expectations of the school system are they likely to be ready to experiment with more effective ways of teaching any content area. The findings of this study suggest that further work needs to be done in the behavior of first-year teachers and how this behavior relates to pre-service teacher education programs.

A somewhat surprising but interesting finding of the survey was that while the school districts in this study did not provide special support for innovative programs in mathematics, neither did a great deal of opposition exist to prevent teachers from using methods deemed effective and appropriate instead of assuming that the school system is the sale culprit in preventing innovation and change, teacher educators might very well look to their own programs as a source of trouble.

Because of the small sample and the low rate of return, the findings are tentative but lend support to the dropout factors as a model that deserves further investigation. Additional testing of the model using a larger sample and classroom observation needs to be done using the Jencks-Peck approach to mathematics education.

References

Jencks, S. & Peck, D. Symbolism and the world of objects. The Arithmetic Teacher, 1975, 22 (5), 317-371.

Jencks, S. & Peck, D. Building mental inquiry in mathematics. New York, Holt Rinehart and Winston, 1968.

Chapter 8

The Relationship between Type of Teacher Reinforcement and Student Inquiry Behavior in Science*

CLIFFORD H. EDWARDS

MICHAEL BURMA

Introduction

It has long been assumed and demonstrated in numerous studies that reinforcers which are associated with particular behaviors produce at increased frequency of these behaviors. Recognition of the power of reinforcers to influence and shape behavior has persuaded many teacher educators to encourage trainees to develop patterns of praise as a simple means of eliciting appropriate behavior from their students. In addition, to be sure, parents use the same patterns of praise to encourage desirable responses from their children. It is assumed that this is the basic reason why Rowe (1974) found in her study that praise and mimicry (mimicry is a pattern of reinforcement where student verbal responses are parroted back by the teacher) seem to be habituated in the speech of many teachers.

* From Journal of Research in Science Teaching, 1980, 17(4), 337-41. Copyright© 1980 by the National Association for Research in Science Teaching. Reprinted by permission of John Wiley & Sons, Inc.

In Rowe's research, it was discovered that verbal praise and mimicry were associated with a decrease in the frequency of inquiry behavior in science by elementary school children. Such a finding obviously has enormous implications for teachers in many areas, but particularly for teachers of science, where inquiry constitutes a substantial part of the curriculum effort. Rowe states that it may be more advantageous to allow intrinsic rewards to drive inquiry, especially since verbal praise apparently does not and since intrinsic rewards are more likely to be suited to the intentions of the learner. Rowe goes on to explain how Pritchard (1969) has shown that overpayment in terms of rewards decreases attention to task. Rowe concluded that extrinsic rewards draw attention away from the task and encourage focus on competition for rewards and concern for equity.

This analysis tends to distort somewhat the potential use that can be made of extrinsic reinforcers. The findings of Rowe seen reasonable if extrinsic rewards are limited to short verbal statements of praise and mimicry. However, there is a whole range of reinforcers with demonstrated potency that needs to be explored in relation to inquiry. Reinforcement theory generally indicates that if a particular stimulus is genuinely reinforcing, it will increase the incidence of the behavior it is associated with (Bijou & Baer, 1961). In the case of short verbal statements of praise and mimicry, these reinforcers are given as rewards for short student responses, thus encouraging these responses to occur. In other words, verbal praise and mimicry encourage the display of short student responses and discourage inquiry because they are given as contingencies for the short responses and not inquiry. The problem is whether a reinforcement system designed to make inquiry truly dependent upon appropriate contingencies of reinforcement can increase the frequency of inquiry or if reinforcement per se limits the incidence of inquiry.

The purpose of this study was to determine the effect on inquiry of two different contingencies of reinforcement. The first of these was using the ideas and input by students in the inquiry process by integrating them into the lesson and referring to them again periodically as appropriate. This is called "using student ideas" and is the first of two independent variables. The second reinforcement approach was to reward inquiry behavior with tokens being used as generalized reinforcers with a variety of backup reinforcers. This is a second independent variable. It was hypothesized that tokens as well as the practice of using student ideas in the inquiry process would increase the frequency of inquiry responses by students. Student inquiry responses constituted the dependent variable.

Method

Subjects

Subjects ((Ss) for the study were four intact groups (25-30 per class) of biology students primarily at the sophomore level in high school. Ss self-selected themselves into various classes based on normal scheduling constraints and thus were assumed to be in somewhat random placements, with all groups essentially equal. The school was a laboratory school where a deliberate effort is made to insure that the total student population is a true cross-section of the community. The same teacher taught all four classes and altered his behavior to correspond to the appropriate treatment.

Experimental Design

The design was a posttest-only design with a control group and involved the use of intact groups. However, all groups were essentially equivalent on the criterion measure prior to treatment in that almost no student inquiry behaviors could be noted in any of the groups. It was assumed that this was likely due to the pre-treatment behavior of the teacher, which consisted primarily of using mimicry and verbal praise as reinforcement.

Each of the four groups was randomly assigned to one of four treatments. Group 1 received verbal reinforcement and mimicry exclusively as a treatment. Verbal reinforcement consisted of praise given verbally by the teacher for student responses which he deemed appropriate to the class discussion. Mimicry is defined as the teacher parroting back the correct response of the student immediately following the response.

Group 2 received the treatment of extending and using student ideas as a reinforcing function. In this instance, the teacher attempted to incorporate the student's response into the lesson by allowing these ideas to help provide direction for the lesson. Student ideas were explored in more depth and referred to subsequently by the teacher when they appeared to have relevance to the subject being discussed. Particularly, student inquiry responses were used and explored by the class.

Group 3 was exposed to a token reinforcement system using special privileges as backup reinforcers. Tokens were dispensed when students engaged in inquiry behavior.

Group 4 was the control group and the treatment consisted of the teacher providing no verbal reinforcement and carefully avoiding reinforcing students in the form of extending and using their ideas.

Statistical analysis included an F-test followed-up by Scheffe procedures to determine the significance of the differences of means between the control group and the various treatments and between treatments.

Procedure

No special instructions were given to Group 1. In this treatment the teacher provided verbal reinforcement and mimicry at an average rate per class period of 12.88 instances of verbal reinforcement and 54.94 instances of mimicry. Five days were allowed for applying this procedure to insure a stable rate of student response to this treatment.

Again, no special instructions were given to Group 2. Here, the teacher provided reinforcement by extending and using the ideas of students in the inquiry process. This was accomplished by his focusing attention on the student responses that were central to the inquiry process. To do this, the teacher explained to the class how the student response fit into subject consideration. These ideas were then used as points for discussion and served as the basis for direction in the inquiry process. The average instant of verbal reinforcement and mimicry during data collection was 3.91 per class period.

The treatment given to Group 3 was a token reinforcement system. Students were told they would be given tokens as a consequence of making inquiry responses and that these tokens could be exchanged for a number of backup reinforcers. These backup reinforcers consisted of special privileges suggested by the teacher as well as additional reinforcers suggested by the students themselves. This list included (1) being able to play a game during the subsequent period, (2) being excused from class early, (3) adding points to a grade, (4) being the teacher's lab assistant, (5) being given free time, and (6) being able to run projectors. There was an average of 4.05 instances of mimicry and verbal reinforcement per class period during data collection.

Group 4, the control group, received no special instructions. The teacher was instructed to eliminate the use of verbal reinforcement and mimicry which was part of his verbal pattern. A period of about 10 days was required to reduce the instance of verbal reinforcement and mimicry to below 10 for a full class period. An additional 5 days were allowed for applying this procedure before data were collected. During data collection the average instance of verbal reinforcement and mimicry was 1.87 per class period.

Data Collection

The dependent variable consisted of the measure of inquiry responses made by students. These included (1) questions by students of an inquiry nature, (2) alternative explanations, (3) suggestions for new experiments, and (4) sharing ideas between students and between students and teacher. In addition, the length of the student response was considered to be associated with inquiry, but was treated separately because it by itself could not be considered to be an inquiry response. These categories of inquiry are consistent with those utilized by Rowe (1974), with the exception of inflected speech, which again was considered by the authors to accompany inquiry but not be an inquiry behavior per se. The categories were thus considered to have construct validity.

All classroom sessions were recorded on audiotape. Student and teacher responses were coded and recorded in 3-second intervals for the entire class period during tape analysis. All different responses occurring during a 3-second interval were recorded. If a response lasted longer than 3 seconds, it was recorded for each 3-second interval that it lasted. The 3-second interval was used based on the experience of Flanders (1970) in his interaction Analysis System, where similar types of behavior were coded and recorded. The following categories of behavior were observed and recorded: mimicry (M), verbal reinforcement (V), using student ideas (U), student inquiry responses (I), questions by the teacher (Q), structuring and conveying information by the teacher (), student response to a question by the teacher (R), teacher responses to student inquiry (R-t), silence or confusion (Si), and controlling responses by the teacher (C).

One-fourth of the tapes were checked for interrater reliability. Scores ranged from .79 to .93. Average reliability was .84.

Results

The research question was to determine if reinforcement per se reduces the frequency of inquiry behaviors of high school biology students or if various reinforcers differentially affect inquiry responses. Three different types of reinforcers were used. The first was verbal reinforcement and mimicry (1), the second, using student ideas (2), and the third was a token reinforcement system (3). Group 4 was the control group, where there was an absence of reinforcement. The analysis of variance was the statistical technique used. This was followed up by Scheffe post hoc procedures.

The results of the analysis of variance for the different treatments are shown in Table 8.1. The F ratio of 25.15 is significant beyond the .001 level.

Table 8.1
Analysis of Variance for Reinforcement Treatments

Source of Variation	Sum of Squares	Degrees of Freedom	Mean Square	F
Between groups	12,106.80	3	4035.60	25.15*
Within groups	3,690.16	20	160.44	
Total	15,796.96	23		

. p .001.

The Scheffe values were as follows. The value for treatment 1 (mimicry and verbal reinforcement), as compared to treatment 2 (using student ideas), was 37.95. Treatment 1, as compared to treatment 3 (token reinforcement), produced a value of 65.45. Treatment 1 versus 4 (control group) had a Scheffe vallue of 24.9. The Scheffe value for treatment 2 compared to treatment 3 was 3.76; treatment 2 versus 4 was 9.61; and treatment 3 contrasted with treatment 4 was 9.30. The critical value at the .05 level of confidence is 9.30, at the .01 level is 14.82 and at the .001 level is 24.3. Thus two contrasts exceeded the .05 level while another three exceeded the .001 level of confidence. Only the contrast between treatments 2 and 3 was not significant.

The length of student response was also studied for each of the four groups. Group 1 had a mean response length of 3.34 seconds. For Groups 2, 3, and 4 it was 6.12, 6.11, and 7.43, respectively. For Group I only 5 student responses exceeded 3 seconds in length. None exceeded 12 seconds. Group 2 had 39 student responses exceeding 3 seconds while Group 3 had 24 and Group 4 had 20.

Discussion

The results of the study help to verify the outcome of Rowe's (1974) study, which indicated that verbal reinforcement and mimicry are related to a reduced frequency of inquiry in science. In fact, the results show that less inquiry results from the use of mimicry and short verbal reinforcers than from no reinforcement at all. However, as hypothesized, the same relationship does not hold for other contingencies of reinforcement. It cannot, therefore, be concluded that reinforcement has a negative effect on student inquiry behavior, but rather that it is a function of the nature of the reinforcement. The results of this study indicate that inquiry behavior can be significantly increased through reinforcement based on the utilization of student ideas in the instructional process as well as through reinforcement in the form of tokens with appropriate backup reinforcers.

These findings have important implications for the science teacher. As pointed out by Rowe, a good deal of teaching is accompanied by verbal reinforcement and mimicry. Such behavior on the part of the teacher is counter-productive in terms of inquiry by students, having the opposite effect to the one intended. Because mimicry appears to be habitual rather than deliberate, teacher training efforts in science and other areas which foster inquiry need to insure that teachers undergoing training learn to bring their behavior under conscious control. That means that in addition to breaking the mimicry habit, teachers need to learn patterns of reinforcement that do encourage inquiry. Using student ideas as defined in this study is one of these patterns. Abandoning mimicry and supplanting it with skills in using student ideas will likely be a difficult training task if the experience in this study is any indication. Yet such alterations in teaching patterns will be required to bring about increased student inquiry.

References

Bijou, S.W., & Baer, D.M. Child development 1: A systematic and empirical theory. New York: Appleton-Century-Crofts, 1961.

Flanders, N.A. Analyzing teaching behavior. Reading, Mass.: Addison-Wesley, 1970.

Pritchard, R.D. Equity theory: A review and critique. Organizational Behavior and Human Performance, 1969, 4, 197-211.

Rowe, M.B. Relation of wait-time and rewards to the development of language, logic and fate control: Part II-rewards. Journal of Research in Science Teaching, 1974, 2, 291-308. (Manuscript accepted October 29, 1979.)

Chapter 9

The Research Problem—Conditions to Help in Selecting a Problem

- Some problems don't have a scientific determination—answer to question can't be found except philosophically, eg. Question: Should high school boys work? This question is philosophical and not subject to scientific definition. To be investigated, it has to be subject to a criterion—eg. do high school boys who work suffer academically from it?

- Tentative ideas have to be converted into a precise researchable problem. It must be stated in precise terms or operationalized. Only then can collection of data have direction, and required answers be sought through analysis.

- To be of scientific value—a concept must be defined in terms of an empirical referent—eg. Learning must be defined in terms of *measurable* changes in pupil behavior. The study must specify the basic operations to get at what is relevant to the solution—eg. is teacher effectiveness to be evaluated in terms of supervisor ratings or on the basis of pupil progress as measured on standardized achievement tests? eg. Problem: The role of the principal in American public education. Restatement: Differences in the supervisory practice of principals in large and small elementary schools of a city.

Problem: The value of a remedial reading program at the college level. Restatement: The effects of a remedial reading program on the academic achievement of a county junior college freshman.
Step #1 is problem selection.
Step #2 is the derivation of one or more hypotheses as to its likely solution.

A hypothesis can be considered a tentative generalization concerning the relationship between two or more variables of critical interest to the problem studied. It is an assumption that has to be tested, especially, in cause and effect relationships. They provide direction and bridge the gap between the problem and the evidence needed for its solution. They act as a framework for the conclusions. They guide the direction of relevant data and provide a structure for meaningful interpretation in relation to the problem under investigation.

- Theory is a fertile source of hypotheses. Reasoning deductively from theoretical premises, we can hypothesize that if x is true then x' must also be true (or at least worth testing). And so an hypothesis is simply an educated guess, a proposition placed "on the table" where its validity can be tested or in other words, the relationship postulated can be either confirmed or refuted.

- This is done in two stages: as stated—the hypothesis allows the investigator to develop deductively certain logical implications that, when stated in operational terms, can lead to the rejection of hypotheses that are in logical conflict with accepted knowledge. For example, the hypothesis that corporal punishment is an effective motivational technique against crime would have to be questioned in that it contradicts long standing findings concerning the relative ineffectiveness of punishment as an incentive.

If the hypothesis passes logical agreement then it must be subjected to an empirical test through the collection and analysis of new data bearing logically on the hypothesis. Example: the hypothesis that being firstborn is conducive to vocabulary development can be verified through the measurement of the vocabulary of firstborns and their later born siblings.

And so—first you postulate a research hypothesis relating to the expected outcome or relationships among variables: Example: first graders with Head Start experience will outperform comparable children without such experience.

- To test the validity of the research hypothesis—sometimes in experimental designs the NULL hypothesis which, in effect says,—no, there is no relationship here; the difference between the groups is simply a matter of chance. This may be the opposite of what you believe and it is often proposed with the expectation that it will be rejected. You then proceed to test this null hypothesis and if the data in question cannot be accounted for on the basis of chance—they apparently reflect a relationship so proposed in the research hypothesis.

We can never prove (or verify) a hypothesis by producing factual evidence that is in harmony with it. Confirmation of it simply raises the level of confidence we can place in it—always a matter of probability.

- A hypothesis that is sustained by logical or empirical tests provides the basis for a generalization or conclusion.

- Pertinent to research are statistics of inference research is generally conducted on the basis of a sample from which generalizations concerning the population are reached. More specifically, the investigation computes certain sample values as a basis for inferring what the corresponding population values might be; Example: the principal might calculate the average IQ for a 10% sample of the student population as the basis for estimating the average IQ of the whole school.

- And so while descriptive statistics relate only to the particular group for which they were calculated, statistics of inference attempt to generalize beyond the particular sample to the population which this sample represents.

- The purpose of statistics of inference is to help isolate differences that are real from those that are due to chance fluctuation. The pos-

sibility has to be considered that obtained results have simply occurred through the chance effects of random variables, a hypothesis
that must be subjected to statistical tests.

Null Hypothesis

The logic underlying such a test revolves around the probability or im-
probability of the occurrence through chance of a difference of the mag-
nitude of that obtained. If the difference is so large that it makes such an
event very improbable, the null hypothesis is rejected, in favor of the
more plausible rival hypothesis. Example: if group A decisively outper-
forms group B. it can be concluded that method A is more effective in
promoting pupil growth than is method B.

•   The rejection of the null hypothesis in this case is tantamount to
    assuming the superiority of one method over the other. If, on the
    other hand, the difference is so small that its occurrences on the
    basis of chance is relatively probable, the null hypothesis is "ac-
    cepted", with the understanding that chance could account for such a
    difference. All that is said is that chance is an acceptable explanation
    of the difference obtained. The null hypothesis is never proved or
    disproved; it is simply accepted as plausible or rejected as implau-
    sible. What is being tested is not whether there is a difference be-
    tween the two samples—this is obvious from the data—but whether
    there is a real difference in the populations that the two samples
    represent—for example, in the methods under comparison.

Structuring Your Research Activities

The planning stage of your research involves important decisions about
procedures which will determine the worthiness and validity of the final
product of the research process—an answer *to the problem question.*

•   The problem question refers to that refinement of the felt difficulty
    (the indeterminate situation—the one you don't have any answer to)
    into a clearly presented question which the researcher wants to an-
    swer. That answer becomes the output of the research process. The

first major decision that must be made in regard to the problem is based on getting an answer to the questions is this a problem that is researchable? Before the answer to this question can be obtained other questions must be attended to:

1. Is the answer already known? (Related Literature)
2. Can the solution to the problem be determined from objectively obtained data and/or information?
3. Are there any ethical aspects which would preclude carrying on the study?

• If the answer to the question is known, the time and money spent on a research project would be wasted. A scientific approach to the solution of the problem assumes that the information needed can be obtained objectively and organized meaningfully for interpretation.

• The consideration of ethics is important because of the human subjects involved in most educational research. A point that has already been made—inanimate objects can be studied in almost any way without fear of permanent damage, but studies of human beings must be carefully checked to see that the subjects under study are not affected adversely by any procedure or treatment that involves such subjects.

Problem Presentation

It is next to impossible to answer the questions that I have posed and to proceed with the process without a well-developed problem to provide direction. Early classification of the felt difficulty is best attained by *writing* a *question*, keeping in mind that the *answer* is the object of the research. The direction toward a solution will rest on a well-developed and delineated formulation of the problem. When the question is established, the direction of the study becomes clearer.

• "A question well-stated is a question half-answered."
• "A well-defined, manageable problem results in a well-defined manageable study."

- One major way to narrow down your problem is to read sources which give overviews or summaries of the current status of research in your area.

  Here is where related literature comes in with references such as the *Review of Educational Research* and the *Encyclopedia of Educational Research.*

- In narrowing the problem down you should select an aspect of the general problem area which is related to your area of expertise. For example, the general problem area, "the use of reviews to increase retention" could generate many specific problems such as "the comparative effectiveness of immediate versus delayed review on the retention of geometric concepts" and "the effects of review games on the vocabulary words of second graders." Some caution here is appropriate—a problem too narrow is just as bad as a problem which is too broad. You do want to contribute to the science of education.

Sources of Problems

You could go to theory because there are many educationally relevant theories such as theories of learning and behavior from which problems can be drawn. Theory contains generalizations and hypothesized principles which should be subjected to investigation. This might be a bit too "heavy" for beginning researchers.

Another source of problems for investigation is the researchers' *personal experience.* It is hard to imagine a teacher or counselor who hasn't had a hunch concerning a better way to do something (for example, a way to increase learning or improve behavior.) The literature is also a good source of problems. In addition to overviews and summaries (as in abstracts) which are helpful in narrowing down a problem area, specific studies often suggest "next step" studies which need to be conducted. A study could either be extended or repeated in a different setting in order to establish its generalizability.

Characteristics of a research problem: 1) it should be a "researchable" problem or one that can be investigated through the collection and analysis of data; 2) it should have theoretical or practical significance, 3) it should be a good problem *for you.* It should match your current level of research skill/resources/time and other restrictions. For example: subjects and measuring instruments are important considerations.

Problem Statement—should define all relevant variables. These can be defined either directly or operationally—operational definitions define concepts in terms of operations or processes. An excellent source of definitions is the Dictionary of Education.

An example of a problem study might be: "The problem to be investigated in this study is (or "the purpose of this study is to investigate") the effect of positive reinforcement on the quality of English compositions. The variables to be defined are "positive reinforcement" and "quality of English compositions." Positive reinforcement might be defined in terms of positive written comments such as "good thought" and "much better". The quality of the compositions might be defined in terms of such factors as number of complete sentences and number of words spelled incorrectly. In the example, the relationship to be investigated between the variables is cause-effect, the purpose of the study is to see if positive reinforcement (the cause) influences the quality of compositions (the effect).

Building Researchable Problems

Researchable problems are listed on the left-hand side of the page, comments about what is wrong with each in the middle, and suggested improvements, right. In the final examples, the aid becomes an exercise.

Researchable Problem	Comments	Revised Problem
1. Students in our school system cannot really read well.	•This takes a position but that's OK. •"Really" has no research answer. •"Well" is a value judgment unless carefully defined. •Suggesting directionsfor change could be helpful.	Are students in our school system reading at grade level? If not, what can be done to improve reading scores?

2. What can we do about desegregation?	•"Do about" is a term that means different things to different people	How can our community prepare for the possible effects of court-ordered school desegregation?
3. Why is the curriculum in our school so bad?	•The researchable problem takes a position but does so based on a term "bad" that cannot be defined except in a value judgment.	Directions for change: Evaluating the curriculum at our school.
4. Parents should be more involved in school-related decisions.	•Once again, the problem is the value judgment "should" •"School-related" is vague.	You revise.
5. Why do school board policies so frequently follow the recommendations of the superintendent? Is the school board at all responsive to other groups besides the school administration?	•Too long and wordy •Unclear about whether or not the superintendent and administration should be considered as one.	You revise.
6. What is the ideal way to teach reading?	•Can't be answered by evidence.	You revise.
7. Why is discipline so poorly handled at our highschool?	You comment	

Elements of a Research Proposal

Ch. I The Problem
- Intro and Background
- Statement of Prob Situation (need, concern)
- Purpose (goal oriented)—Practical outcome
- Questions to be answered
- Statement of Hypothesis (educated guess)
- Importance of study (may overlap with problem situation)
- Definition of terms
- Delimitation (narrowing of focus)
- Outline of what is to follow

Ch. II Review of Related Literature
- Overview of organization of two chapters
- Acquaint reader with existing studies
- Establishes poss. need for study (likelihood of obtaining new data)
- Significant results—should be from last ten years
- Include unpublished studies—e.g., dissertations
- Summary of literature reviewed (brief)

Ch. III Methodology
- Description of method or approach to be used (Descriptive, Questionnaire, Interview, Experimental, Pilot Study, data collection—selection of subjects (sample)
- Instrumentation (tests, measures quest.)
- Data collection
- Data processing and analysis
- Limitations

Ch. IV Analysis and Evaluation
- findings presented in tables, etc., when appropriate
- findings reported with respect to furnishing evidence to support or contradict hypothesis
- factual information kept separate from interpretation. (ties together finding in relation to theory or lit. review or rationale)
- Summary

Ch. V <u>Summary/Conclusions/Recommendations</u>
- Brief summary of that covered in first three chapters and in findings of Ch.IV.
- Conclusions ("so what" of findings) often the hypothesis is restricted to its general ability)
- Recommendations (practical suggestions for implementation of findings or additional research)

Once again, you will be guided best to an effective investigation by remembering that a question well-stated is indeed a question half-answered.

A Survey Technique

The mailed Questionnaire (a tool of research) is the most widely used technique in education. It requires a careful, clear presentation of the problem underlying the questionnaire. Otherwise—ambiguity and mis-interpretation will invalidate the findings. "A question well-stated is a question half-answered."

Three key terms for your questionnaire—goals, clarity, credibility.

Construction:
A. Often planned poorly or overdone. There is a problem of "consumer resistance to overcome" and so they should be done as skillfully as possible and introduced with reasons justifying their existence.
B. State the reason for the questionnaire and explain how information will be analyzed. Avoid wordiness and ambiguity.
C. Objectivity is important. Lengthy subjective or open-ended answers are difficult for the respondent to write and for the investigator to evaluate. If possible, categories of response can be anticipated. These should be offered as alternatives to an objective question. For example:

Do you have a systematic program for identifying gifted children in your school? YES _____   NO _____

If yes, what means of identification do you use?

a. Group IQ test   d. aptitude battery
b. Individual IQ test   e. teacher ratings
c. achievement battery   f. other (specify)

D. One of the best ways of developing good objective questions is to administer an open-ended form of the question to a small sample of subjects representative of the population in which you are interested. These lengthy answers provide the data from which to derive your objective type answers.
E. Questions should eliminate unnecessary steps for you; should help minimize the problems of evaluation and interpretation of answers.
F. Avoid questions that are threatening to the respondent/that expose him to criticism /or place him in an awkward position (sometimes anonymity counteracts these.)
G. Avoid questions which provoke bias in the response or obscure objective information. For example:

How do you rate your guidance program?
Excellent/Good/Average/Fair/Poor.

H. Avoid leading questions.
I. Pretest the questionnaire. How?
1) Select a sample of the population the questionnaire is eventually aimed at.
2) Provide space for respondents to make reactions and suggested changes.
3) Use the pretest questionnaire under the same conditions you think will prevail at the time of the final study.
4) Check percent of responses as an estimate of what might occur in the final run/examine the returned trial questionnaires for trouble signs, such as items left blank or that are of little informational value/misinterpretations or ambiguity. Check the comments for similar indications.
5) Analyze the results to assess the effectiveness of the trial questionnaire for desired information.
6) Make appropriate additions, deletions, and modifications to the questionnaire. (Example: if answers to a particular question show sharp disagreements or raise further questions,— additional clarifying questions may be necessary.)

7) Overall reaction of subjects to questionnaire—what did they like/dislike/want modified?

The Letter of Transmittal

1. **Purpose**: to get back the maximum number of *returned* questionnaires.

2. **General Characteristics**: a clear/brief/adequate statement of the purpose and value of the questionnaire.

3. **Effectiveness**

    a. It must provide good reason for the subject to respond/should involve him in a constructive and appealing way/his sense of responsibility/intellectual curiosity/personal worth should be appealed to.
    b. It should establish a reasonable but firm return date.
    c. Possibly an offer to send the respondent a report of the findings (should be carried out).
    d. If possible, use a letterhead and signature that will lend prestige and official status to transmittal letter.

4. **The Follow-up Letter**
    A few days after the deadline established in letter of transmittal. The tone of the letter—respondent had intended to return questionnaire but perhaps overlooked it.
    •   should reaffirm importance of the study.
    •   value of individual's contribution to this important study. National Education Association reports the following return rate for questionnaires:
    A first follow-up at 13 days after deadline yielded 63.4%/ 27 days yielded 83.6%/37 days yielded 96.8%.

5. **The Problem of Non-Responding Subjects**
    There will always be a percentage of non-respondents.
    The question has to be asked: "How would the results of my questionnaire be changed if all subjects had returned the questionnaire?"

*Over 20% raises questions about the "hold-outs" and what they are withholding. For example, there is a common bias that persons having a good program are *more likely* to respond than persons having a poor program.

*Correction for this—randomly select a small sample of the non-respondents and personally interview them to obtain the missing information. Disadvantage—time consuming and expensive.

6. **Effect of "Anonymity"**
   Designed to encourage honest and frank answers. This is more likely when aimed at personal or controversial information. The disadvantage—conceals information about respondents that might be of interest in analysis. (Example: sex, age, geographic position, etc.) Studies show that there is little difference in answers by adults for signed and unsigned questionnaires.

Appendix A: An Author's Critique

"Head Start"—The Development of Skills, Experience, and Abilities in Kindergarten Children

1. Question

A ccording to the investigator, "The purpose of this study was to evaluate whether the children who participated in Project Head Start were better prepared for kindergarten than those who did not participate. . .". To accomplish this purpose, the investigator: 1) reviewed the literature, 2) stated hypotheses, 3) selected subjects, 4) selected and constructed measuring instruments, 5) administered and scored tests, 6) performed data analyses, and 7) drew conclusions.

What two importantly different kinds of information are contained in the review of the literature? What, in general, are the main purposes of any review of the literature and how well did the investigator succeed in achieving these purposes?

1A. Answer

One kind of information in Kaplan's literature review is the description of the social and political forces which in 1965 were changing drastically the pre-kindergarten public education of economically and socially disadvantaged children. The Kaplan report indicates that by 1965 Project Head Start "benefited" 560,000 youngsters in 2,500 communities at an estimated cost of $112,000,000. A second kind of information in the literature review is more commonly found. The investigator cites empirical studies (e.g., Bernstein, 1960, 1962; Deutsch, 1956b) and studies of new educational practices (Graham and Hess, 19651 Hess and Rosen, 1965).

One main purpose of a review of literature section in empirical studies is to describe the educational context in sufficient detail such that the justification of the study is clear. The literature review succeeds fairly well in giving us the political, historical, and empirical context of the study. These political and social changes in educational practice which the investigator documents serve as an excellent stimulus and justification for educational research.

A second main purpose of a review is to indicate the source of concepts and principles used to guide the inquiry. One can find instances in which the evaluation was influenced by empirical studies and writing quoted in the review, one example of the influence of these sources on the conduct of the inquiry is the literature which points to the need for emphasis on language teaching for the disadvantaged. This information justifies the inclusion of language development measures in the study.

A third main purpose is to provide a theoretical context from which the knowledge claims of the inquiry can receive intelligible interpretation. There is none of this material in the review. Some readers would say that the large differences found after a short summer program are rather remarkable, yet there is no theoretical context, nor even an educational rationale provided which can help us to account for or make sense out of these findings.

#1. Hypotheses

The "Hypotheses" presents a clear statement of the questions to which the investigator is seeking answers. Although it is not always necessary for questions to be in the form of hypotheses in which predicted results are stated, we approve of the investigator's indication in this section of the direction in which she predicts the results will appear. Most experts favor directionally stated scientific hypotheses to those expressed in the less communicative null form.

In assessing the hypotheses, several student readers questioned the investigator's methods of measurement, the failure to consider other variables in the study, and the feasibility of matching students. Valid as these concerns may be, for convenience they will not be considered at this point in our assessment of the study.

#2. Subjects

The principal technical flaw in the evaluation is that *no control* was exercised over the *assignment of children* to Head Start or control programs. Further, because such variables as sex, ethnic background age (only a 10-month range), language spoken in the home, and age of siblings would not be expected to be highly correlated with the measures used in the study, the reader has little assurance that the two groups being compared were initially equal in those skills and abilities the Head Start program most wanted to affect. The investigator also mentioned this problem.

We could assess more accurately the likelihood of this initial equality if we were told in the report the reasons why the control children did not attend Head Start classes. Did they live too far away from the Head Start center, come from more stable homes, or live in better neighborhoods? Did the control children not attend Head Start Programs because their parents chose not to send them? If so, then differences in attitudes toward education (as seen by differences in the learning experiences provided in the home-learning experiences such as talking, reading, color identification, etc.) could mean that the Head Start children would have scored higher than the control children even before the Head Start experience was begun and certainly after an additional year of a better learning situation in the home.

The investigator was wise not to match students on intelligence or other cognitive or attitude variables measured after the Head Start experience. If the Head Start program improved the children's scores on such variables, then matching children on their scores would cancel the very effects to be demonstrated.

Suppose the investigator had been able to administer identical criterion measures (verbal fluency, enunciation, etc.) before the Head Start experience and to match children on the basis of their scores on such measures. Differences between the two groups would still be expected on these measures when the children were tested in kindergarten, even if the Head Start program had no effect in developing the skills and abilities measured by the criterion tests. Such bogus or false differences can be explained by the regression phenomenon.

We do not fault the investigator for matching students. We merely wish to point out that such matching was probably largely ineffective in assuring the equality of the two groups prior to training. Matching on variables measured before the Head Start programs were begun and which were more highly related to the criterion variables would have been far preferable. But even if this were done, the lack of random assignment of children to the Head Start and control conditions still prevents the ruling out of selection bias and regression effects.

Frequently expressed reactions of student readers are that 55 children per group is too small a number and the number of Head Start programs being evaluated is not mentioned in the article. More data are always desirable, but an investigation must weigh the increased scope against the increased "costs" associated with having a larger sample size. The differences between the Head Start and control groups were sufficiently great that 35 cases per group were adequate to reject for most of the variables the "chance alone" null hypothesis. Perhaps more useful than a larger sample size would be having as a sample children taken from several Head Start programs. We suspect, but are not certain, that all the children were exposed to the same program and, if this was the case, the generalizability of the results is very uncertain.

#3. Measuring Instruments (Selection and Construction)

Given the rather limited goal of assessing the comparative performances of the two groups of children, then ideally the measuring Instruments used in the study should represent a diverse collection of reliable and valid devices for measuring the degree to which the intended skills and abilities have been developed and undesirable unintended ones are absent.

Many student readers objected to the absence of test reliability and validity data in the report. If a test is unreliable, then it is not measuring any trait or skill consistently; the test score then has a large component of random error. Such inconsistency of measurement and random error are to be avoided since real treatment effects are obscured by such unreliable instruments. In the context of this study, Head Start programs cannot be judged effective if the measures of effectiveness are largely unreliable. Since the investigator did find group differences, we can assume that the instruments employed had at least sufficient reliability to demonstrate what was desired.

"Narrowly considered, validation is the process of examining the accuracy of a specific prediction or inference made from a test score. . . . One validates, not a test, but an interpretation of data arising from a specific procedure." The investigator would probably claim that the test items are representative instances of the skills being described and, thus, her inferences about children's capabilities based on their test performance are valid. Such a claim seems reasonable to us with possibly two exceptions. First, we question whether the Goodenough Draw-a-Man Test is as much a measure of motor coordination as it is an indicator of other skills. Second, we have some slight qualms about the buttoning-own-clothes measure since the task is not the same for all children. (Some children had clothes harder to button than others.)

Because the specific Head Start programs being evaluated were not described, we do not know for sure the extent to which the abilities and skills measured by the tests used in this study represent the primary objectives of these programs. Further, we do not know the extent to which the very tasks used in the tests were used in the training programs themselves. This is not to say that it would be wrong to use identical tasks in both teaching and testing. It is just that interpretation of group differences and the value of a program depend upon knowing the relation of tasks tested to the tasks used in training.

We suggest that in an evaluation study of this type three categories of tasks be used in the testing: (1) those tasks directly involved in the training (on which large group differences favoring the Head Start group would be expected); (2) tasks not used in the training but on which it is hoped there will be group differences; and (3) tasks representing unintended outcomes (on which there are no particular expectations).

We wished more of the category two and category three tasks were used in this evaluation. As examples of category two tasks, we would like to have seen the differences in performance of the two groups on tasks requiring left-right visual search and production of graphic symbols (e.g. letters). In addition, as a category two or three task, measures of personal social adjustment to school would have also been of interest.

The investigator is to be commended, however, for including several measures of performance rather than relying on just one or two. Where there were no standardized tests to measure the type of performance on which the investigator wished to compare the groups, she devised her own tests for these skills and abilities. This, too, is commendable.

#4. Test Administration and Scoring

The importance of administering tests prior to the start of the Head Start program was mentioned earlier.

The investigator indicated that the instruments were administered, ". . . at the beginning of kindergarten in order to insure that these skills and abilities to be tested were not learned during the kindergarten experience. Although there is some merit to this procedure, we feel it would have been desirable if some of the tests had also been administered at the end of kindergarten, or even later. The critical importance of ascertaining the long-term benefits of Head Start program has been well documented by the investigator herself. The advantage of the Head Start group during the first weeks of the school year may be due primarily to preschool environment and materials which have no carry-over effect on later learning. Although determining if there is an immediate effect is useful, it would be of great value to document that a primary goal of Head Start programs, increased performance in school, was met.

Recall that the measuring was not blinded from the standpoint of the observer, although the investigator claims to have made no effort to remember which children were in the Head Start group. This is small comfort to the reader who suspects that the children's membership in either group could have been independently identified and thus could have biased the judgment of the investigator as she administered and scored the tests.

The testing was somewhat subjective, both in administration (e.g., frequency of directions to be given, probing for termination of responses) and scoring. (See especially, the cutting, coloring, and enunciation tests.) Thus, the results were open to the influence of the evaluator herself. The investigator is not to be faulted for using instruments which were subjective in nature. However, using these instruments in such a manner that the subjective element invalidates the comparison between the two groups is a procedure open to criticism.

#5. Analysis

The analysis of the data was adequate and not misleading even though more precise statistical techniques could have been employed. The investigator could have utilized the exact scores and not have forced them into two categories (above and below the combined median). Further, the investigator could have made use of the fact that she had matched pairs of children. However, these objections carry little weight since the result of substituting these more refined techniques would have been more power (i.e., likelihood of rejecting false "no difference" hypotheses) and almost all of the chance-alone or no difference hypotheses were rejected even without their use.

The investigator is to be commended for not evidencing an unthinking attachment to a particular criterion of statistical significance. Particularly in the case of the cutting skill variable, the evaluator showed her willingness to accept evidence of a difference even though the obtained test statistic fell somewhat short of the critical value needed to claim statistical significance at the 5 per cent level.

#6. Investigator's Conclusions

The investigator is quite correct in stating that, ". . . kindergarten children who had attended the Head Start program were superior to those who had not in each of the skills and abilities tested." This conclusion is merely a factual statement of the results found. Even though a few differences did not reach statistical significance, it is a fact that the Head Start group had superior scores on all the measures.

The investigator is also permitted to say, "The findings support the current view that culturally deprived children benefit from preschool programs." "Findings support the current view" is interpreted to mean that the findings are consistent with the current view, and it does not imply that the results prove that the children benefited from the programs.

Because of the lack of fundamental controls as specified earlier in our appraisal, we have no assurance that the differences were due to the Head Start programs. Thus we feel the investigator is not justified in making conclusions that imply the Head Start programs caused the superior performance. We question the validity of such a conclusion as: "The experiences provided in the instructional program made it possible for children in the preschool Head Start project to become more adept. . . .".

Finally, before claiming that results will generalize to other Head Start projects, we would want to see such positive results from a larger sample of students and programs.

2. Question

The investigator evidently feels that the Head Start programs involved in her study were very effective and worthwhile. Yet there is information needed in addition to that given in the report if one is to reproduce such an effective program elsewhere. What information is lacking in the report which prevents it from serving as a guide to one who must develop and operate a Head Start program? (Assume that the leader has much freedom in how be plans and runs a Head Start program.)

2. Answer

To develop and operate a Head Start program effectively, one would need to have much financial, legal, and political information not touched upon in the report. To plan the instructional aspects of the program, that is, to decide what to teach and how and when to teach it, a detailed specification of the Head Start programs being evaluated in the present article is needed. Lack of this specification is a major deficiency of this report.

The reader is left completely in the dark as to the components of the programs, their duration, the training and number of staff, the objectives of the programs, the procedures used to achieve these objectives, and so on. Without even the most rudimentary description of the programs, the investigator has produced an evaluation report not unlike a research report in which the independent variable was unspecified. As the report now stands, its nearly total neglect of description of the programs makes it of use only to a small number of persons who are intimately acquainted with the programs being evaluated. No two Head Start programs are alike. Without a description of the programs herein evaluated, we do not know what programs to perpetuate or how the programs should be conducted differently. What good is an evaluation that something works when that "something" is an enigma?

Appendix B: An Author's Critique

The West End—An Urban Village

On the Methods Used in this Study

The Purposes and Methods of the Study

The findings of any study are intrinsically related to the methods used to develop them. Although this study may be described generally as based on participant-observation, a more detailed description of the methods is necessary to indicate the overall perspective of the research, and some shortcomings of the findings.

Findings are also affected by research purposes. I had two major reasons for making this study: a desire to understand neighborhoods known as slums, and the people who live in them; and a desire to learn firsthand what differentiates working-and-lower-class people from middle class ones. These questions were based partly on my concern about middle-class bias in the planning and caretaking professions.

Having been trained in sociology at the University of Chicago during the era when Everett C. Hughes and the late Louis Wirth—to name only two—were dominant influences in the Department of Sociology, I believe strongly in the value of participant-observation as a method of social research. As a result, I felt I could best achieve my study purposes by living in a slum myself.

---

* Source: Abridged from Herbert Gans, Urban Villagers (New York: Free Press, 1962,) pp. 336-350.

133

Although I had wanted to do the study for several years, other projects had prevented my searching for a suitable area. Consequently, I was very pleased when I was offered the opportunity of making a study in the West End—a particularly suitable neighborhood. Not only was it known as a slum, but it was also a white area, and thus somewhat easier for a white participant-observer to enter. For while the method is difficult to use when it requires a trip across class barriers, it is much more so when racial barriers also exist. Much as I would have liked to do the study in a black slum, I doubted at the time whether many blacks would have accepted a white participant-observer in their midst. The West End was also attractive because it was adjacent to the North End, the district described in William F. Whyte's classic Street Corner Society. Not only were my purposes based on some of the same values that guided his study, but my belief in the desirability and feasibility of the project had also been much encouraged by his book, as well as by the detailed description of the way in which he went about his study.[1]

My actual field work employed six major approaches:

1. Use of the West End's facilities. I lived in the area, and used its stores, services, institutions, and other facilities, as much as possible. This enabled me to observe my own and other people's behavior as residents of the area.
2. Attendance at meetings, gatherings, and public places. I attended as many public meetings and gatherings as I could find, mostly as an observant-spectator. I also visited area shops and taverns in this role.
3. Informal visiting with neighbors and friends. My wife and I became friendly with our neighbors and other West Enders, spending much time with them in social activities and conversations that provided valuable data.
4. Formal and informal interviewing of community functionaries. I interviewed at least one person in all of the area's agencies and institutions—talking with directors, staff members, officers, and active people in settlement houses, church groups, and other voluntary organizations. I also talked with principals, ministers, social workers, political leaders, government officials—especially those concerned with redevelopment—and store owners.

5. Use of informants. Some of the people I interviewed became informants, who kept me up-to-date on those phases of West End life with which they were familiar.[2]

6. Observation. I kept my eyes and ears open at all times, trying to learn something about as many phases of West End life as possible, and also looking for unexpected leads and ideas on subjects in which I was especially interested.

The data which evolved from the use of these methods were written down in field notes, and placed in a diary. They were subsequently analyzed for this report.

The Types and Problems of Participant-Observation

The first three of the methods I used are usually described under the rubric of participant-observation—a generic and not entirely accurate term for a variety of observational methods in which the researcher develops more than a purely research relationship with the people he is studying. The actual types of participant-observation which I used, and the problems which I encountered, therefore deserve more detailed consideration.

Variations in the participant-observation method can be described in different ways. One principle of classification is the extent to which the researcher's participation is known to the people he is studying. That is, whether it is kept secret, revealed partially, or revealed totally.[3] I have found it more useful to classify the approaches in terms of differences in the actual behavior of the researcher. This produces three types:

1. Researcher acts as observer. In this approach, the researcher is physically present at the event which he observes, but does not really participate in it. Indeed, his main function is to observe, and to abstain from participation so as not to affect the phenomenon being studied—or at least, to affect it no more than is absolutely unavoidable. Much of my participation was of this type, when I was using the area's facilities, attending meetings, or watching the goings-on at area stores and taverns.

2. Researcher participates, but as researcher. In this case, the researcher does become an actual participant in an event or

gathering, but his participation is determined by his research interests, rather than by the rules required in the situation he is studying.[4] For example, in social gatherings, the researcher may try to steer the conversation to topics in which he is especially interested. In such instances, he might be described as a "research-participant."

3. Researcher participates.[5] In this approach, the researcher temporarily abdicates his study role and becomes a "real" participant. After the event, his role reverts back to that of an observer—and, in this case, an analyst of his own actions while being a real participant. For example, he may go to a social gathering as an invited guest and participate fully and freely in the conversation without trying to direct it to his own research interests. Afterwards, however, he must take notes on all that has happened, his own activities included. Needless to say, even during the most spontaneously real participation he can never shed the observer role entirely, if only because he knows he will write it all down later.

In attending meetings and other public gatherings, I acted as observer. In using the West End's facilities, I was usually a real participant, sometimes a research-participant or observer. The informal visiting with friends and neighbors employed a mixture of real and research participation. Given the short time I had for field work, the research participation role turned out to be most productive. The real participation was most enjoyable, but it turned out to be a time-consuming approach. Also, while it is most useful when the object of study is a single group or institution, it is less so in a general community study. Although being a real participant allows the researcher to understand the functioning of a group like no other method can, it also cuts him off from other parts of the society which are studying one political party to study the opposition party as well.

In using these three types of participant-observation, I encountered several problems which deserve some consideration: the difficulty of entry into the community; the identification with the people being studied and doubts as to the ethics of the approach.

The problem of entry into West End society was particularly vexing. As the West Enders were a low-income group, they had neither been interviewed by market researchers nor been exposed to the popular sociology of the slick magazines. Subsequently, they were unfamiliar with the methods and goals of sociology. Also, they were suspicious of middle-class outsiders, especially so because of the redevelopment threat. As a result, I was somewhat fearful at the beginning whether I would be able to function as a participant-observer once I had told people that I was a researcher.

The Center for Community Studies on whose staff I served had already made contact with one of the settlement houses, and the workers, being middle-class, were willing to be interviewed and to help out in the study. They also referred me to some of their loyal clients, but these, I soon found out, were in several ways unlike the large majority of West Enders. Nor did any of these resemble "Doc," the man whom William F. Whyte had met at the start of his study and who had offered to guide Whyte into the society of the North End.[6] Although the early weeks of the study were indeed anxious ones, I did not waste them, using the time to interview the staff members of West End institutions and the officers of its organizations. Eventually, however, the problem almost resolved itself, this time by the same sort of lucky accident that had befallen Whyte. My wife and I were welcomed by one of our neighbors and became friends with them. As a result, they invited us to many of their evening gatherings and introduced us to other neighbors, relatives, and friends. These contacts provided not only pleasant companionship, but a considerable amount of data about the workings of the peer group society.

As time went on, I became friendly in much the same way with other West Enders whom I had encountered at meetings or during informal interviews. They too introduced me to relatives and friends, although most of the social gatherings at which I participated were those of our first contact, and their circle.

After I had been in the area for about three months, I became a familiar face, and was able to carry on longer conversations with storeowners and other West Enders. Finally, the entry problem disappeared entirely. Indeed, I was now faced with a new one: having more data than I could ever hope to analyze.

Even my most notable failure in gaining entry produced useful information, feeling that I should not limit myself entirely to being with people who spent their evenings at home, I decided to do some research in the area taverns. After making the rounds of the West End bars and finding most of them a haven for older men and Polish or Irish West Enders, I finally chanced on one which served as a hangout for a group of young Italian adults of the type that Whyte called "corner boys." From then on, I visited there only. But as much as I tried to participate in the conversation, I could not do so. The bar, though open to the general public, was actually almost a private club: the same dozen or so men came there every night, and—since some of them were unemployed or not working during daylight hours—during the day as well. Moreover, I suspect that some of them were engaged in shady enterprises. In any case, they were extremely loath to talk to strangers, especially one like myself who came unintroduced, alone, and then only irregularly about once a week. Also, much as I tried, I could not really talk about the subjects they covered or use the same abundance of four-letter profanity. After several unsuccessful attempts, I gave up trying to intrude and sat quietly by, from then on, as an observer. As it turned out, however, I learned a lot from listening to their conversations and to their comments about the television programs that they watch intermittently.

One of the factors that complicated the entry problem was my initial desire to be only an observer and a Teal participant, that is, to gather data simply by living in the West End and to learn from the contacts and conversations that came my way just by being there, I soon found that this was impossible. There were simply too many questions that I could not ask in my role as an ordinary—and newly arrived—resident. Given the short time I had in which to do the research, I could not wait for these questions to come up spontaneously in the conversation.

Consequently, I told people that I was doing a study of the neighborhood, especially of its institutions and organizations. I also sensed quickly that they were familiar with historical "studies," and thereafter described my research as being a recent history of the area. The revelation of my research role ended a few relationships, but on the whole, it helped my study and made it easier for me to approach people with unusual questions.

In addition, I wanted initially to refrain from interviewing as much as possible, except among people such as agency staff members and organizational leaders who were used to it. I made this decision partly on epistemological grounds—doubting whether I would get trustworthy data—and partly because I was not sure that I could be both interviewer and participant-observer in the same neighborhood. When I found I was not gathering enough data, I changed my mind, and, subsequently, I did interview a number of West Enders. But this was always done quite informally and without a questionnaire, except one lodged firmly in my memory. I did no door-to-door interviewing, however, partly because I did not like to do it, and because I found it difficult to assume the detached role of the interviewer who comes as a stranger, never to be seen again. Although I never considered myself to be a West Ender, I did think myself to be enough of a participant in the life of the area to feel uncomfortable about also being an interviewer.[7]

A second problem of participant-observation is that of identification with the people one studies. Every participant-observer becomes emotionally involved not only in his study, but also with the people, since it is through their willingness to talk that he is able to do his research. And this involvement does have some advantages: it allows the observer to understand the people with whom he is living, and to look at the world through their eyes. At the same time, it can also blind him to some of their behavior patterns, and thus distort the study.[8]

The identification is probably more intense if the people being studied are suffering from deprivation, and if they are a low-status group whose point of view is not being taken notice of in the world outside. In such a situation, the researcher feels a need to do something about the deprivation, and to correct false stereotypes about the people. This reaction also befell me. I quickly became convinced that the redevelopment of the area was unjustified, and that the planning was being poorly handled. This identification can be socially useful—at least from the liberal perspective—for the sociologist then becomes an informal spokesman for groups who themselves lack the power to voice their demands in a larger society.

Although identification can detract from the objectivity of the research, it need not do so—especially if the researcher knows what is happening to him. Moreover, the identification, likely to be strong at the beginning, decreases in intensity as the research proceeds. It is reduced even further in the time which elapses between the end of field work, the data analysis, and the writing of the report. Instances of overidentification in the field work can therefore be dealt with in later stages of the research. In my case the dangers of identification were somewhat reduced by their being channeled largely into the redevelopment issue, a topic peripheral to the main purposes of my study. Thus, I expressed my identification with the West Enders through my critique of the redevelopment process, and was able to remain more detached about the social structure and culture of the West Enders.

The dangers of overidentification are also reduced by the many differences between the researcher and the people he is studying. Since the researcher is an observer more often than he is a real participant, he is always conscious of value clashes when they occur during the field work. Thus, while the participant observer cannot argue with his informants and respondents as fully as he would like—because it might endanger his rapport—he is continually made aware of his own points of view on the subjects that come up in conversation. This not only produces insights useful to his research, but also keeps him detached from the people he is studying. He realizes that he cannot be like them, or that he should not even try to be.[9] At the same time, he becomes ever more sensitive to the fact that values arise out of the social position of those who hold them. Thus, when the researcher becomes a spokesman for the people he is studying, he is really arguing with those who fail to see this basic sociological fact. This accounts for the intensity of my reaction about the narrow-mindedness of the world at large and my dismay at the middle-class professional who expects people to share his own values even though they lack the opportunities and cultural background that have shaped his own views.

The third problem of the participant-observer approach concerns its ethical validity. Although I did tell people that I was in the West End to make a study, I described my research mainly as a survey of organizations, institutions, and the redevelopment process. I mentioned but did not stress my interest in studying the everyday life of West Enders, and did not mention at all that I attended social gatherings in the dual role of guest and observer, at the time I felt sure that this admission would either have ended the relationships, or have made life so uncomfortable for them and for me that I could not have been either guest or observer. With some hindsight and additional participant-observation experience in another community, I feel now that I could have been more open about my role. Most people are too busy living to take much notice of a participant-observer once he has proven to them that he means no harm, ·

The fact that I was using friendly relationships for the collection of data, coupled with my feeling that I was thus exploiting these relationships, did create some guilt. My feelings of anxiety were somewhat alleviated, however, by the fact that my study was based neither on harmful or malicious ends. Needless to say, I had intended from the start to maintain the privacy of my informants. Thus, I have used no names in the report, and have frequently distorted facts that would make it possible for West Enders to recognize their erstwhile neighbors. In attributing quotes, I have freely used the term "neighbor" as a synonym for West Ender, and some of the people I have quoted were not really neighbors at all.

Although these explanations and safeguards do not solve the ethical problem of whether the ends of the study justified the means used in making it, I can see no easy solution to this problem. The social scientist attempts to describe the world as it is, and he must therefore observe people in their normal, everyday ways. Should he hide his purpose, either by not telling them of his participant-observation role, or by asking interview questions which get at more than they seem to on the surface, he does so because he has no other alternative. If he bares all his research purposes, he may be denied access to the very society he wants to study. If he forswears participant-observation and gathers his data solely by interviewing, he can get only reports of behavior, but not behavior itself. If he is completely open about his participant-observation or interview questions, his respondents are likely to hide information from him—not necessarily by intention—by giving him access not to behavior but to appearances; not to what people do, but how they would like their doings to appear publicly.

If research methods do involve some evasion, the social scientist is saddled with a great responsibility to the people he has studied. The researcher must try to prevent any harm from coming to the people he has studied, either from his research or its publication. There is one exception: if the people studied are participants in what appears to the researcher as a gross miscarriage of justice, he has the right to publish his conclusion, even if the correction of the injustice might hurt them. Because these requirements force the researcher to set himself up as a judge over other human beings, he must take personal responsibility for these decisions and for the hurts his study could cause. Beyond that, he must be as objective as is humanly possible, not by renouncing value judgments, but by refraining from hasty and oversimplified ones, and by showing why people behave as they do, especially when this behavior violates prevalent norms.

All these precautions, of course, cannot do away with the fact that research, like all other human activities, is political; that it supports one point of view and vested interest at the expense of others.[10] The researcher must therefore take a political stand on some issues, and he should make it clear where his sympathies lie. This I have tried to do.

The Analysis of the Data and Some of Their Limitations

The actual analysis of the data was quite simple. I recorded my observations and interviews as soon as possible after they had been completed, together with the generalizations they stimulated, and placed them in a field diary. When I came to write the study, I read and reread my diary several times, and then put the generalizations and some supporting observations on index cards. Eventually, I had more than 2000 of these. I then sorted and classified them by a variety of subject headings. The classification was determined in part by my initial research purposes, in part by topics in which I had become interested during the field work, and in part by the observations made spontaneously while in the field. The content of the cards was then further digested into pages of notes listing the major generalizations and other ideas. An initial report was written from these notes in 1959.[11] Before I wrote this present version, I reread the diary and took further notes on it.

The study is based on quite simple—if not primitive—research methods, and its findings are hypotheses. Moreover, what evidence I have offered for them is illustrative rather than documentary. This is not accidental; from the start I had decided to give lower priority to methodological sophistication than to the search for hypotheses. I tried, of course, to be a careful observer, and a careful analyst of what I had observed, but I did not attempt to seek evidence for my hypotheses on a systematized basis. As a result, the findings have several limitations.

Many of the generalizations of the study fall into the category of what Merton has called "post factum sociological interpretation" in that they have been developed after the observation. Concerning this, Merton has warned:

> A disarming characteristic of the procedure is that the explanations are indeed consistent with the given set of observations. This is scarcely surprising, inasmuch as only those post factum hypotheses are selected which do accord with these observations. . . . Post factum explanations remain at the level of plausibility (low evidential value) rather than leading to "compelling evidence" (a high degree of confirmation). Plausibility . . . is found when an interpretation is consistent with one set of data. . . . It also implied that alternative interpretations equally consistent with these data have not been systematically explored, and that inferences drawn from the interpretation have not been tested by new observations.[12]

Merton's criticism can be applied to my own findings. I did try, however, to guard against overly facile interpretation by analyzing my data immediately after collecting them, and by putting both data and analysis into the field notes. Thus, I developed interpretations at once, rather than at the end of the study. This gave me an opportunity to test these notions in later observations. Since I did not begin the study with a set of explicit notions that I wanted to prove at all costs, it was not difficult to surrender poor interpretations for better ones. Most of the generalizations reported were thus developed during the field work.

Participant-observation also has another major drawback—the size and quality of the sample on which observations are based. Although my study sought to report on a population of close to 3000, I probably met and talked with no more than 100 to 150 West Enders.[13] Moreover, my most intensive contact was with about twenty West Enders, and most of my hypotheses about the peer group society are based on my observations of their ways. Because of the size of my sample, I did not attempt any statistical analysis. Nevertheless, I have used freely such quasi-statistical terms as "many," "most," "some," or "the majority of." Obviously, my use of these concepts is based on impressionistic evidence.[14]

Also, I could not determine to what extent any reported behavior pattern or attitude was distributed throughout the population, nor could I inquire into subgroupings and subcultures among the West Enders, other than the most obvious ones of class and age. Even then, I did not apply the distinction between action seeking and routine-seeking West Enders as fully as I might have. Thus, while the report may state that the West Enders act in a certain way, or hold a given attitude, only more extensive research will be able to indicate whether my generalization applies to all of the second-generation Italians in the West End, or only to certain subgroups among them.

The West Enders with whom I had the most intensive and most frequent contact were drawn more from working-class routine-seekers and mobile people than from the lower-class action-seeking population. Although I did have many opportunities to observe the latter, and to hear their actions discussed, they were harder to reach directly and therefore were reached less often in the time I had for field work. Moreover, some of the people I encountered were marginal to the peer group society, and for this reason were most cooperative with me. Conscious of the bias in my sample, and knowledgeable enough about the West End to evaluate the information I received from the marginal people, I was able to take these considerations into account when I analyzed my data. This does not, however, entirely eliminate the distortion due to lack of contact with the West Enders who are lowest on the educational and socio-economic level. Consequently, the findings should be read with the reminder that I did not report as fully about the people for whom life was hardest, and for whom the outside world was most threatening.

Finally, more of my data were gathered from and about men than women. As I noted in my description of the peer group society, communication between the sexes is much more difficult than in middle-class society. Even though my wife participated in the field work and told me about the female social gatherings, my report does tend to place greater emphasis on the male portions of the peer group society.

This, then, is not a scientific study, for it does not provide what Merton has called compelling evidence for a series of hypotheses. It is, rather, an attempt by a trained social scientist to describe and explain the behavior of a large number of people—using his methodological and theoretical training to sift the observations—and to report only those generalizations which are justified by the data. The validity of my findings thus rests ultimately on my judgment about the data, and of course, on my theoretical and personal biases in deciding what to study, what to see, what to ignore, and how to analyze the products. Properly speaking, the study is a reconnaissance—an initial exploration of a community to provide an overview—guided by the canons of sociological theory and method but not attempting to offer documentation for all the findings. In making this statement, I do not mean to cast doubt on the conclusions I reached—I stand behind them all—or on the methods I used. Participant-observation is the only method I know that enables the researcher to get close to the realities of social life. Its deficiencies in producing quantitative data are more than made up for by its ability to minimize the distance between the researcher and his subject of study.

Notes

1. "On the Evolution of Street Corner Society," in William F. Whyte Jr., *Street Corner Society*. Chicago:University of Chicago Press, 2nd ed., 1955, pp. 279-358.

2. Anthropologists use informants to get basic information about the culture they are studying. I used them mainly to get data about specific institutions in which they were functioning, and to check observations or impressions gathered in my field work.

3. This principle has been used by Raymond L. Gold, "Roles in Sociological Field Observations," Social Forces, vol. 36 (1958), pp. 217-223; and by Buford H. Junker, Field Work, Chicago: University of Chicago Press, 1960, Chap. 3.

4. He must, of course, follow the rules that guide participation in the event, or he will be ejected. For example, he cannot tell people to stop talking about a topic that does not interest him.

5. These three types cut across what Morris and Charlotte Schwartz have described as passive and active participation. See their "Problems in Participant-Observation," American Journal of Sociology, vol. 60 (1955), pp. 343-353, at pp. 348-350.

6. Whyte, op.cit., p. 291.

7. I did, however, help to pretest the interview schedule being used by the larger study, and interviewed, without discomfort, an ex-West Ender who had left the area some years earlier.

8. Morris and Charlotte Schwartz call this affective participation, and indicate how it can be dealt with. Op. cit., pp. 350-352.

9. I did not wear the middle-class uniform of suit, white shirt, and tie, however, in order to minimize my connection with the hospital that was sponsoring the research in which I was involved. Its support of the redevelopment program had antagonized many West Enders. I did not try to look like a West Ender but one day, while wandering through the area, some college students who were taking pictures there treated me—literally—as if I were a native. Their tone of well-meaning condescension made me see more clearly than ever why West Enders harbor uncomplimentary feelings toward the middle class.

10. For a clear statement of this fact, see John R. Seeley, "We Hidden Persuaders: Social Thought and Politics," an address to the National Federation of Canadian University Students, McMaster University, 1961, mimeographed. My conclusions about the ethics of participant-observation have benefited from discussions with him and with Fred Davis.

11. "The Urban Villagers: A Study of the Second Generation Italians in the West End of Boston." Boston: Center for Community Studies, November, 1959, mimeographed.

12. Robert K. Merton, Social Theory and Social Structure, New York: The Free Press of Glencoe, 2nd ed., 1957, pp. 93-94.

13. I include in this number neither the middle-class caretakers, nor other people working in West End or with West Enders: they were not West Enders.

14. Howard S. Becker and Blanche Geer have developed new methods of participant-observation and data analysis which remove some of the dangers of post-factum interpretation, and make it possible to quantify data gathered by this method. Their methodological innovations are reported in Howard S. Becker, "Problems of Inference and Proof in Participant Observation." American Sociological Review, vol. 23(1958), pp.652-660; and in Howard S. Becker and Blanche Geer, "The Analysis of Qualitative Field Data" in Richard N. Adams and Jack J. Preiss, eds., Human Organization Research, Homewood, Ill.: Dorsey Press, 1960, pp. 267-289. The field study in which these methods are applied is reported in H. Becker, B.Geer, E. Hughes, and A. Strauss, Boys in White: Student Culture in Medical School, University of Chicago Press, 1961.

References

Becker, H., Geer, B., Hughes, E., and Strauss, A. 1961. *Boys in white: Student culture in medical school.* Chicago: University of Chicago Press.

Becker, Howard S. 1958. Problems of inference and proof in participant observation. *American Sociological Review*, 23: 652-60.

Becker, Howard S., and Geer, Blanche. 1960. The analysis of qualitative field data. *Human Organization Research*, Richard N. Adams and Jack J. Preiss, ed. 267-289.

Bijou, S.W., and Baer, D.M. *Child development 1: A systematic and empirical theory.* New York: Appleton-Century-Crofts, 1961.

Center for Community Studies. 1959. *The urban villagers: A study of the second generation Italians in the West End of Boston.* November.

Chicago State University. 1961. *Chicago schools journal*, December: 122-27.

Davis, Allison. 1948. Social class influences on learning. *The Inglis Lecture.* 29-30.

Flanders, N.A. *Analyzing teaching behavior.* Reading, Mass.: Addison-Wesley, 1970.

Gans, Herbert. *Urban villagers.* New York: Free Press, 1962.

Gold, Raymond L. 1958. Roles in sociological field observations. *Social Forces.* 36: 217-23.

Issac, Stephen, and Michael, William B. *Handbook in research and evaluation.* California, edits, 1977.

Jencks, S., and Peck, D. 1975. Symbolism and the world of objects. *The Arithmetic Teacher*, 22 (5):317-71.

Jencks, S., and Peck, D. *Building mental inquiry in mathematics.* New York: Holt, Rinehart and Winston, 1968.

147

Junker, Buford H. *Field work*. Chicago: University of Chicago Press, 1960.

Merton, Robert K. *Social theory and social structure*. New York: The Free Press of Glencoe, 2nd ed., 1957.

National Association for Research in Science Teaching. 1980. *Journal of Research in Science Teaching*. 17(4):337-41.

Pritchard, R.D. 1969. Equity theory: A review and critique. *Organizational Behavior and Human Performance*. 4: 197-211.

Rowe, M.B. 1974. (Manuscript accepted October 29, 1979.) Relation of wait-time and rewards to the development of language, logic and fate control: Part II—rewards. *Journal of Research in Science Teaching*. 2: 291-308.

Schwartz, Morris and Charlotte. 1955. Problems in participant-observation. *American Journal of Sociology*. 60:343-53.

Seeley, John R. 1961. We hidden persuaders: Social thought and politics. An address to the National Federation of Canadian University Students at McMaster University, mimeographed. My conclusions about the ethics of participant-observation have benefited from discussions with him and with Fred Davis.

Toynbee, Arnold J. 1957. *A Study of History*, abridged ed. New York: Oxford University Press. vol. 11.

Whyte, William F. Jr. 1955. On the Evolution of Street Corner Society. *Street Corner Society*. Chicago: University of Chicago Press, 2nd ed.: 279-358.

Young, Michael and Willmott, Peter. *Family and kinship in East London*. London: Routledge and Kegan Paul, 1957.